MW01703486

Foreword

This Exam Preparation guide is intended for those preparing for the GIAC Security Essentials Certification (GSEC) with a broad networking focus.

The Art of Service is an Accredited Training Organization and has been training IT professionals since 1998. The strategies and content in this book are a result of experience and understanding of the GSEC, and the exam requirements.

This book is **not** a replacement for completing a course. This is a study aid to assist those who have completed an accredited course and preparing for the exam.

Do not underestimate the value of your own notes and study aids. The more you have, the more prepared you will be.

While it is not possible to pre-empt every question and content that may be asked in the GSEC exam, this book covers the main concepts covered within the GSEC discipline.

Due to licensing rights, we are unable to provide actual GSEC Essentials Exams. However, the study notes and sample exam questions in this book will allow you to more easily prepare for a GSEC Essentials exam.

This second edition has been fine-tuned according to your feedback.

Good luck with your exam!

Ivanka Menken

Executive Director

The Art of Service

Write a review to receive any *free* eBook from our Catalogue - $99 Value!

If you recently bought this book, we would love to hear from you! Benefit from receiving a free eBook from our catalogue at http://www.emereo.org/ if you write a review on Amazon (or the online store where you purchased this book) about your last purchase!

How does it work?

To post a review on Amazon, just log in to your account and click on the Create your own review button (under Customer Reviews) of the relevant product page. You can find examples of product reviews in Amazon. If you purchased from another online store, simply follow their procedures.

What happens when I submit my review?

Once you have submitted your review, send us an email at review@emereo.org with the link to your review, and the eBook you would like as our thank you from http://www.emereo.org/. Pick any book you like from the catalogue, up to $99 RRP. You will receive an email with your eBook as download link. It is that simple!

Table of Contents

GIAC Security Essential Certification

The GIAC Security Essential Certification (GSEC) is provided by the Global Information Assurance Certification (GIAC). It covers several major topics of information security and is similar in scope to CISSP, GISP, and SANS Information Security.

The topics covered include:

- Access Control Systems and Methodology
- Telecommunications and Network Security
- Security Management Practices
- Applications and Systems Development Security
- Cryptography
- Security Architecture and Models
- Operations Security
- Business Continuity Planning and Disaster Recovery Planning
- Law, investigations and Ethics
- Physical Security.

Exam Specifics

GSEC Exams must be proctored and a partnership exists with KRYTERION. Locations of test sites can be obtained at http://www.giac.org/proctor/kryterion.php. Tests are conducted at a testing center. Registering for the certification must be done first and the process can reviewed at http://www.giac.org/information/schedule_proctored_exam.pdf.

The GSEC exam consists of 180 questions. The candidate has five hours to complete the exam. A minimum passing score of 70% is required.

Exam Prerequisites

There are no prerequisites for the GSEC exam. Renewal can be done every 4 years.

Access Control Systems and Methodologies

Access Control Theory

Security programs depend on the ability to control access to systems, services, resources, and data. Controlling access requires the ability to identify, authenticate, authorize, and monitor who or what is accessing the assets of an organization.

Confidentiality, integrity, and availability are fundamental principles guiding access control solutions.

Access controls are a set of mechanisms working together to protect the assets of the enterprise. They encompass all aspects and levels of the organization. Management uses access controls to:

- Determine who accesses a system
- Determine what resources are accessed
- Determine what operations can be performed
- Establish accountability.

Principles of Access Control

An access control policy ensures appropriate decisions are made related to user identification and authorization and the level of access to resources provided. A policy provides consistency to the provision, management, and administration of controls.

Some common security policies include:

- Separation of duties

- Least Privilege
- Information Classification.

Separation of Duties

The purpose of separating duties is to prevent errors and fraud by disseminating tasks and privileges for a specific process across multiple users.

To successfully separate duties, each element within a process or work function should be defined. Separation of duties can be static or dynamic. Static separation assigns individuals to specific roles and allocates specific elements to those roles. Dynamic separation is based on the course of system operations, by using the process to determine the roles and elements based on the situation.

In applying separation of duties, two factors are considered:

- Sensitivity of function
- Element distribution.

Each job performed has a different criticality based on its exposure to potential fraud, misuse, or negligence of duties. The greater the criticality, the more separate the duties should be.

Not all elements within a function are rated the same or need the same level of attention when implementing security measures. The defining factors are typically:

- The importance and criticality of identified elements

- Consideration for maintaining seamless operations
- The availability of human resources and skills.

Least Privilege

The most important characteristic of access control is the principle of least privilege. A user or process is given only what is required to perform its functions, and using only the resources to support that function. With this restriction in place, undue access to system functions and sensitive data is controlled.

Information Classification

Information classification is a process of evaluating the risk level of information to determine the proper level of protection required. Security controls applied to information is impacted by:

- Cost of time
- Cost of people
- Hardware
- Software
- Maintenance.

Benefits to classifying information include:

- Creating organizational awareness
- Identifying information required for business recovery
- Establishing information value
- Providing direction of handling sensitive information
- Focusing investments on resources appropriately

- Establishing information ownership
- Providing review and approval processes
- Ensuring greater security for highly sensitive information
- Establishing requirements of information and their locations
- Reducing expense of inefficient storage.

To establish a data classification program:

1. Determine project objectives
2. Establish support from organization
3. Develop classification policy
4. Develop classification standards
5. Develop classification process flow and procedures
6. Develop tools
7. Identify application owners
8. Identify data owners
9. Distribute templates
10. Classify information
11. Developing auditing procedures
12. Load information
13. Train users
14. Review and update classification periodically.

All information needs to be marked and labeled with the appropriate information classification. To ensure that the classifications are being used properly, periodic testing should be performed.

Access Control Architecture

The access control architecture consists of:

- Categories of access control
- Types of access control

Control Categories

Categories allow access control characteristics to be mapped to control types. Six main access control characteristics are:

- Preventative – avoiding incidents
- Deterrent – discouraging incidents
- Detective – identifying incidents
- Corrective – applying remedies
- Recovery – restore conditions to normal
- Compensation – alternative control.

Prevention of potential incidents is typically handled by restricting the activities of users. Though access may be provided to a system, privileges define what can be done on the system by the user.

Deterrents such as the identification and authentication of a user, service, or application, attempt to minimize the frequency and impact of incidents.

Properly implemented access controls provide visibility into the access environment, such that incidents can be identified and tracked for evidence or alerts. Visibility is provided by:

- Intrusion Detection Systems (IDS)
- Virus controls
- Applications
- Web filtering
- Network operations
- Administration
- Logs audit trails.

Corrective activities usually occur after security incidents and focus on identifying the actions required to prevent the incident or impact from reoccurring. Corrective actions can also be a result of identifying weaknesses in security.

Unlike corrective activities which focus on the recurrence of an incident, recovery activities attempt to compensate for the sake of returning to normal operations after an incident.

Compensating controls are used when existing capabilities do not support the requirement of a policy. These controls can be technical, procedural, or managerial.

Types of Controls

Three types of access control exist:

- Administrative
- Physical
- Technical.

Administrative describes the activities defining the roles, responsibilities, policies, and administrative functions required. All the actions, policies, and management of the control system fall into the administrative realm. There are six major groups associated to the administrative group:

- Operations policies and procedures
- Personnel security, evaluation, and clearances
- Security policies
- Monitoring
- User management
- Privilege management.

Physical refers to the non-technical controls such as locks, fire management, gates and guards. The most prevalent concern is physical entry into a facility and considers:

- Clearing and supervising visitors
- Defining access to controlled areas
- Display of appropriate identification at all times
- Reviewing and auditing access rights and privileges.

Many facilities will have multiple zones defined, with different levels of security applied to them, often contributing to a defense-in-depth solution.

The technical type describes the mechanisms used within the digital infrastructure to enforce the security policy. Technology controls include a combination of firewalls, filters, operating systems, applications, and routing protocols. Different considerations include:

- User controls
- Network access
- Remote access
- System access
- Application access
- Malware control
- Encryption.

Administrative Controls

The policies and procedures associated with access control and security include:

- Change Control
- Business Continuity and Disaster Recovery
- Performance Management
- Configuration Management
- Vulnerability Management
- Product Life-Cycle Management
- Network Management.

Security requirements should include all defined job roles and responsibilities. Roles should be aligned to defined policies and include general responsibilities for adhering to security policies and specific responsibilities for ensuring the protection of associated assets.

Requirements for access control should be defined and documented, usually as rules and rights for each user or group of users. This is typically in the format of a policy which considers:

- Security requirements for individual applications, systems, and services
- Information authorization and dissemination
- Access control consistency throughout different systems and networks
- Contractual and regulatory obligations
- User access profile standards
- Management of the access control system.

Monitoring provides a means of identifying deviations from established access control policies in regards to:

- Authentication processing
- Authentication attempts
- Management of credentials
- Management of users
- Rights usage
- Denial of rights and access.

Monitoring includes activities for logging and reviewing events.

Basic elements of a user management process include:

1. Approval of user to access systems
2. Standard, uniquely defined user IDs, format, and other specifics

3. Checking the level of access is appropriate to the role and job purpose
4. Requiring a signed written statement with condition for access
5. Documenting system changes
6. Providing audits and status of the control environment
7. Corrective action for unauthorized access.

User passwords are a vital component of an access control environment. When governing passwords, consider:

- User agreements to keep passwords safe and confidential
- Temporary passwords can only be used once and must be changed by the user
- Passwords are never stored unprotected or in clear text
- Passwords should have a minimum and maximum length and include various characters and formats
- Passwords should be changed regularly
- A history of passwords should be maintained to avoid repeating old passwords.

Privilege management handles the allocation, administration, and use or rights and privileges in systems. Procedures for privilege management consider:

- Defining the privileges found and mapping them to associated roles
- Managing privileges based on what is required to perform duties
- Defining an authorization process and recording all

privileges allocation

- Assigning extraneous duties for a user to a separate user account.

Technical Controls

User controls are directly associated with the user and typically revolve around authentication factors. The factors represent:

- Something the user knows
- Something the user has
- Something the user is or does.

A single-factor authentication method, such as a username and password combination, focuses on the use of one factor. A two-factor authentication method considers two factors such as a token, fob, or smart device providing a one-time password, certificate, or biometric. All factors are considered in the three-factor authentication and typically utilizing fingerprints, retina scanning, hand geometry, facial features, or keystroking.

The purpose of network access controls are to limit communication and are associated with:

- Access control lists
- Remote-access solutions
- Virtual local area networks
- Protocols
- Firewalls

- Intrusion detection systems
- Intrusion prevention systems.

The intent is to segment, filter, direct or reject communication to and from the network.

Roaming users comprise a large portion of user communities. Remote-access solutions provide services to acquire access to systems and data from wireless points and remote locations. Virtual private networks (VPNs) are a typical solution for controlling remote access and are a combination of authentication with encryption.

Systems can be comprised of a single server or a set of servers providing a service or function. The most common attributes of a system are the server and the operating system. Access controls are typically managed by the operating system and apply to users, file systems, and processes.

The simplest form of system access is on a single system and host; though the most common is access to the file system where access to the system is validated as well as access to the individual files.

Applications utilize user and system access controls to protect from threats and reduce exposure to threats. The ability to protect from attack lies significantly in the architecture of the application. Security can be found in several layers of the application framework.

Technical controls are used to reduce the likelihood of impact from an unwanted influence. The most common control for this purpose is anti-virus solutions. Commonly found on the perimeter of the network, the servers themselves, and on each client station, malware control attempts to compensate for any known or unknown weaknesses in systems, applications, and services.

Encryption, or cryptography, is used to ensure the confidentiality of information or to authenticate the integrity of information.

Management of Access Control

Access controls and strategies are covered over a range of topics, including:

- Identification and authentication
- Access control services
- Identity management
- Access control technologies.

Identification and Authentication

Identification ensures that the person requesting access is associated correctly with the role defined in the system. It is important for managing downstream activities and controls, such as accountability. The purpose of identification is to bind the individual user to the appropriate set of unique rights and privileges to required systems, applications, and services.

A person's identity is verified using authentication methods. When accessing a system, a person presents their unique user identification and additional data to establish trust between the user and the system. This combination can be as simple as a username and password. The system will authenticate the user and grant access if successful.

Common forms of identification include:

- Username
- User ID
- Account number
- Personal identification number (PIN).

Three essential practices for identification include:

- Uniqueness
- Nondescriptive
- Issuance.

Identification for a user must be unique to the individual. A single person may possess several forms of identification, but each of them must be distinct from the others within a system. IDs should expose the role or job function of the user, especially those of:

- Admin
- Administrator
- Webmaster
- Finance
- Root.

In situations where several access control environments exist that do not interact, share information, or provide access to the same resources; it is possible to duplicate the same user identification across those environments. Unfortunately, because individuals are prone to duplicating certain attributes such as passwords, it is typically bad security practice to allow a duplication of IDs.

The process used to issue identities must be secure and documented. The quality of the process will impact the quality of the identifier. An issuance process should consider:

- Approval
- Notification
- Administration
- Allocation.

Authentication can utilize one, two, or all three factors, or types, to verify a user. There are three factors of authentication:

- By knowledge - what a person knows
- By ownership – what a person has
- By characteristic – what a person does or is.

Passwords

Typically, authentication by knowledge is done through a password, a 5-15 string of characters which is remembered by the user and provided with identification when requesting access. The more diverse a password is, the harder it is to crack. Passwords fall into different categories:

- Standard, or dictionary, words are recognizable words that could be found in the dictionary. These are the least secure passwords to be found in a system and are typically not accepted in most systems.
- Combination, or alphanumeric, passwords usually are multiple dictionary words combined with numbers to add complexity.
- Complex passwords will utilize letters, numbers and special characters to create a string. These are the most complex and secure category of passwords, except that their complexity usually will cause a user to write down the password in order to remember it.

Passphrases are an alternative to passwords and follow the same rules as passwords. The difference between the two is that the passphrase utilizes an easily remembered phrase for the user, such as a list of names or a line from a song.

Passwords or passphrases should never be passed over a network or stored in cleartext. The storage of passwords by a system should be protected.

Authentication Devices

Instead of using a password, or in addition to a password, for authentication, a person may have a physical device that can be used for extra security. There are two methods found here:

- Asynchronous token devices utilize a challenge and

response technology requiring interaction between the user and the authenticating party or system. When access is requested, the authenticating party will provide a challenge which can only be answered by the token in possession of the user. The token will provide the correct response which is given to the authenticating party and access is granted.

- Synchronous token authentication is similar in process but relies on an event, location, or time-based synchronization between the requester and authenticating party. The most popular method is time-based where the token utilizes an embedded key to produce a unique string of numbers and/or characters in a given timeframe, usually one minute. The user will enter the character string whenever access is requested to authenticate themselves.

In addition to tokens, authentication devices exist which house the credentials for the user. The two most popular devices are:

- Memory cards
- Smart cards.

The difference between the two is processing power. A memory card will hold information but does not process information. A smart card will process information. A memory card is used like a password to gain access after the user enters their unique ID.

Typically, the process requires the user to present the memory card and a user ID or PIN. If the authentication information on the memory card matches with the user provided information, access is granted. A memory card can be used with computers, but a reader is required to process the information.

The cost of readers, as well as the overhead with generating PINs and cards, needs to be considered in any security solution. These costs need to be balanced with the benefits of implementing memory cards, which is generally, a more secure solution than basic passwords.

Despite this security, memory cards have a basic flaw: the data stored on the card is not protected. The data can be extracted or copied. Since the card cannot process information, the data is unencrypted. Smart cards, on the other hand, can have security controls and logic embedded into its integrated circuits.

A smart card is the size of a credit card and has a semiconductor chip embedded in it. The chip is either a memory chip with nonprogrammable logic or a microprocessor with internal memory. The chip will accept, store, and send information. That information is divided into four sections:

- Information that can be read only
- Information that can be added only
- Information that is updated only
- Information that has no access available.

Integrated Circuit Cards

Smart cards are more correctly termed integrated circuit card (ICC) by the International Organization for Standardization (ISO) to specify all devices which are an ISO 1 identification card with an integrated circuit (IC). The size of the card is 85.6x53.98x0.76mm (the size of a bank or credit card).

The capabilities of a smart card are:

- Ability to store personal information
- A high degree of security and portability
- Tamper-resistant storage
- Security-critical computations isolated within the card
- Secure enterprise-wide authentication
- Use of encryption systems
- Can perform encryption algorithms.

The IC is essentially a memory chip. There are several types of memory that can be implemented into a smart chip:

- Read-only memory (ROM) – the data found in ROM is predetermined by the manufacturer and is unchangeable
- Programmable read-only memory (PROM) – the type of memory can be modified if high voltages are applied to enact links within the IC. Found to be unsuitable for ICC
- Erasable programmable read-only memory (EPROM) – an early implementation operating within a one-time programmable mode (OTP) because of its architecture. To erase the memory, ultraviolet light is required

- Electrically erased programmable read-only memory (EEPROM) – provides user access and can be rewritten many times over. The amount of memory offered ranges from 8 to 256 KB
- Random-access memory (RAM) – with ROM solutions, the data remains intact when power is removed. The opposite is true for cards with RAM, requiring cards to have their own power source. Though the risk is that power will deplete, a RAM card has better storage and speed capabilities.

A microcontroller is integrated into the chip to manage the data in memory. Control logic is used to provide various services, including security. The construction of the IC has great influence on the controls associated with the data.

The configuration of these cards limits certain types of data to be stored on the device, as well as be accessed indirectly from external applications. To allow the card to function as intended and protect the data, programs can be embedded into portions of the memory utilized by the processor.

There are several features that are found in smart cards:

- 64-KB EEPROM
- 8-bit CPU microcontroller
- Cryptographic functions from DES, 3DES, RSA 1024 bit and SHA-1

- 2 to 5.5 V variable power
- 1 to 7.5 MHz clock frequency
- 250,00 to 500,000 write/erase cycles (endurance)
- 7 to 10 years data retention.

How smart cards interact with other systems defines the type of smart cards available. There are two basic types:

- Contact cards require physical contact in order to communicate with other systems
- Contactless cards use proximity technology to provide an interface.

ISO 7816-2 allows eight electrical contacts for a contact ICC to interact with other systems, though only six are used. Each contact (Cn) has a designation starting with Vcc and is embedded counterclockwise around the plate.

Contact	Designation	Use
C1	Vcc	Power connection allowing operating power to the microprocessor
C2	RST	Allows reset signals from the interface device (IFD)
C3	CLK	Clock signal line controlling the operation speed and providing a common framework for data communication
C4	RFU	Reserved for future use

C5	GND	Provides a common electrical ground between the IFD and ICC
C6	Vpp	Programming power connection used to program EEPROM
C7	I/O	Input/output line allowing half-duplex communication channel between the reader and the smart card
C8	RFU	Reserved for future use.

Contactless cards are more durable, have greater speed and convenience and have more applications in use than contact cards. Because they do not require physical contact, less damage is possible to the plate or magnetic strip. Contactless cards are found in devices such as cell phones and PDAs

ISO 14442 defines the physical characteristics, radio frequency power and signal interface, initialization and anticollision, and transmission contactless cards, more commonly referred to as proximity integrated circuit cards (PICC). A low frequency electronic magnetic radiation used to provide power and data interchange. A proximity coupling device (PCD) provides the required signal and power control for communicating with the card. A radio frequency (RF) field is produced by the PCD which activates any card that falls within its electrometric field loop. The field operates at 13.56 MHz ± 7 kHz and constant power range.

The PCD will alternate between tow modulation, or signal, types until a PICC is incorporated into the communication process. Both types, type A and type B, support 106 kbps in bidirectional communications.

The log-on process for smart cards is done at the reader and not the host, providing an advantage to the technology because the identifier and password are not exposed while in transit to the host.

Public key infrastructure (PKI) technologies provide several functions for authentication and information security on smart cards, including:

- Secure log-on
- Secure e-mail/digital signatures
- Secure web access/remote access
- VPNs
- Hard disk encryption.

Biometrics

Biometrics use sophisticated technologies to calculate uniqueness using behavioral characteristics or specific biological indicators of the human body. There are two types of biometrics:

- Physiological
- Behavioral.

Different physiological biometrics include:

- Fingerprints – the oldest form of biometric uses to identify uniqueness

- Hand geometry – draws conclusion by discerning attributes to the user's hand including tension, temperature, length, and width
- Hand scans – combination of fingerprints and hand geometry
- Retina scans – scans the unique attributes of the back of the eye
- Iris scans - scans the colored material surrounding the pupil
- Voice patterns and recognition – determines the unique sounds produced to identify the user in addition to what is being said
- Face scan – verifies the heat signatures and geometry of the user.

Behavioral biometrics focus on determining patterns in a user's actions:

- Keystroke pattern analysis will utilize the user's pin or password along with how the information is entered; driven by the assertion that different people will enter the same information differently
- Signature dynamics will analyze stroke speed, acceleration, deceleration, and pressure along with the content of a user's signature.

Where passwords, tokens, or smart devices offer static processes that have a high level of accuracy and confidence; biometrics are a technical and mathematical-based estimate. Most scans rely on hundreds or thousands of environmental variables to perform an accurate reading. Any variance in those conditions can impact the scan including illness.

There are three categories of biometric accuracy measurements:

- Type I error, or false reject rate, identify when authorized users are rejected as unidentified or unverified
- Type II error, or false accept rate, identify when unauthorized users are accepted as authentic
- Crossover error rate (CER) is the point where the type I and type II errors are equal. The lower the value of the CER, the more accurate the system.

Sensitivity is the key determiner in proper authentication through the use of biometrics. Tuning the system to maintain a low CER is the best way to ensure neutrality.

To maintain the integrity of the control environment, biometrics considers:

- Resistance to counterfeiting
- Data storage requirements
- User acceptance
- Reliability and accuracy.

Access Control Implementation

Typical access control architecture is comprised of three systems:

- Host
- Requester
- Authenticator.

The services found within the architecture support the core attributes of the solution, including:

- Identification – provides identify
- Authentication – verifies identity and associated access
- Authorization – determines what actions are available to the user
- Accountability – tracks user activity.

In security solutions, the host is a system, user, application, or service which provides the interface for identifying and authenticating the user. The requester, network access server (NAS), provides any challenges to the host used to verify the user. The authenticator provides the validation of the user's identity.

Identity Management

A set of technologies used to manage the identities of employees, contractors, customers, partners, and vendors. The IT infrastructure is designed to centralize and streamline the processes for managing the user identity, authentication, and authorization data. All aspects of access control are found within identity management.

Identity management focuses on the provisioning of users, processes, and management of access control. The process typically consists of:

1. Creating a new user profile within the HR database
2. Creating a request for access for the profile
3. The request for access being approved by all necessary managers
4. Approved requests sent to IT teams to grant required access
5. Access granted and recorded in history files.

Challenges to successful identify management solutions include:

- Consistency of user data across multiple systems
- Efficient processes for granting access across multiple systems to reduce repetitive tasks
- Increase of usability by reducing the requirement for multiple prompts to verify identify
- Reliability of user profile data ensures the timely updates of user information
- Scalability of the solution across enterprises.

Identity Management Technology

The technologies used by identity management are:

- Directories
- Web access management
- Password management
- Legacy single sign-on
- Account management

- Profile updates.

Directories are typically a comprehensive system built to centralize data management efforts by containing the data within a hierarchy of objects. A directory can be stored on one or more servers which replicate between themselves. Access to the data in the directory is usually provided by a protocol, such as Lightweight Directory Access Protocol (LDAP).

Directories provide a method for simplifying architectures and avoid replication of information. Unfortunately, legacy systems do not support using external systems, such as directories, to manage users.

Building on directories, data can be leveraged to manage user identity, authentication, and authorization using a web access management (WAM) solution. These solutions typically use a front-end web server to authenticate once when entering the web environment and sustaining that authorization throughout the entire session.

Password management provides a method of tracking passwords across multiple platforms and their various expiration times. Based on the criticality of the application or service, different requirements may exist for resetting or changing the password on a regular basis. Most users have accounts on multiple systems. A password management system can manage the passwords on all these systems and even allow mundane user tasks, such as password resets and account management, to be conducted.

In some cases, a single sign-on (SSO) is provided for users to access one or more systems simultaneously during a single authentication process. In these solutions, a central repository of user credentials is provided, sometimes on a server or within a smart card. These repositories are separate from the application or service being accessed. Therefore some replication process must be in place whenever the user ID and/or password are changed within the application or the repository. Single sign-on solutions have a greater cost attributed to them.

Account management is designed to control the creation, modification and decommission of user accounts within a system. WANs typically manage access control for web-based applications; but not enterprise based solutions. Most account management solutions provide a centralized, cross-platform security capability with features:

- Simultaneous management of user access to multiple systems
- An automated workflow system for submitting requests for new, modified, or deleted accounts
- Automatic replication of data
- Ability to load batch changes to user directories
- Policy-based changes automatically performed to create, change, or remove access
- Focus on enterprise system access.

Profiles are used to identify entities through a collection of associated information. Most profiles will change at some point within the life cycle of the user. Identifying and updating this information in a timely basis is an important aspect of maintaining access control.

Access Control Technologies

Methodologies of Access Control

Methodologies of access control are either centralized or decentralized.

Centralized access control has all access control queries directed to a central point of authentication allowing a single point of administration for the entire system. Examples of a centralized method include:

- Remote Authentication Dial-In user Service (RADIUS)
- Terminal Access Controller Access Control System (TACACS)
- Kerberos.

Decentralized access control is particularly useful where connectivity to a centralized access control system is difficult. Though more difficult to maintain than a centralized system, it is typically less expensive.

One-Time Passwords

A one-time password (OTP) can only be attempted once before it becomes invalid or expires. If the user does not type in the password correctly, the password still becomes invalid and another password must be obtained.

These passwords are not knowledge-based, but token-based (Type 2). They are considered the most secure form of password possible when implemented properly.

The one-time password is based on randomly generated passwords.

RADIUS

Small organizations can generally use the default authentication method of the software providing remote access connectivity. As the organization grows, more sophisticated solutions may be appropriate such as RADIUS or TACACS/TACACS+.

With RADIUS, the access control subject provides authentication credentials to the remote access server which passes the information on the RADIUS Server of authentication. The RADIUS server will respond to the remote access service with either acceptance of the credentials or denial. The key advantage of this system is that the communication between the RADIUS server and the remote access server is encrypted, increasing the overall security position of the system.

A similar procedure to RADIUS is the older TACACS system. The authorization or denial of access is communicated between the TACACS server and the user. There is no encryption used with the TACACS system; however, the TACACS+ system does provide encryption.

Single Sign On Implementations

The purpose of Single Sign On (SSO) is to enable user authentication once and pass that authentication on to each subsequent system that user attempts to access. The most common SSO products are:

- Kerberos
- SESAME
- NetSP
- Kryptoknight
- Snareworks.

The advantages of SSO are:

- Access to systems can be quickly and efficiently enabled or disabled
- The administrative effort for forgotten passwords is reduced
- The experience of the user is improved.

SSO solutions are costly and difficult to implement. Additionally, if a user's password is compromised during an attack, all the systems the user has access to are compromised.

Kerberos

Kerberos is a network authentication protocol providing strong authentication for client/server applications. It uses symmetric-key authentication and authentication tokens, or tickets, to drive the system. Each Kerberos system has a private key and the Kerberos server has copies of all these keys, allowing for cross-platform authentication.

A Key Distribution Center (KDC) holds all the keys and provides a centralized authentication service. The overall structure of control is called a realm. Time-stamping tickets ensure the keys are not compromised. All the systems within the realm have their clocks synchronized to maintain a common reference for authentication.

Part of the KDC is the Authentication Server (AS) which is responsible for authenticating each client. During this authentication, the Ticket Granting Service (TGS) makes the tickets and distributes to the clients.

The process for user logon follows:

1. User identifies themselves by presenting credentials to the KDC
2. The AS authenticates the credentials
3. The TGS issues a Ticket Granting Ticket (TGT) that is associated with the client's token and is valid as long as the user continues the session.

The process for resource access follows:

1. The Ticket Granting Ticket is presented to the KDC with the details about the remote resource being accessed by the client
2. The KDC returns a session ticket to the client

3. The session ticket is presented to the remote resource and access is granted.

Physical Security

Physical security addresses the common risks against the physical and environmental elements where the information system is managed.

Three types of threats to physical security exist:

- Natural
- Utility systems
- Man-made.

Natural threats can range from water leakage and excessive temperatures to disaster.

Utility systems, such as power, can fluctuate or be completely lost as a resource to the organization.

Man-made threats are usually malicious in nature and can consist of physical attack, sabotage, vandalism, arson, or theft.

Some threats are accidental and make up approximately 70% of the attacks by insiders. Most threats and vulnerabilities are from inadequate or lapsed working practices and weak measures for physical security.

Site Location

Site location is a major consideration for determining what physical security precautions are required.

Fabric and Infrastructure

Some concerns for physical security based on the building include:

- Site layout, including entry points
- Building materials used
- Age of the building
- Provision of infrastructure
- Statutory health and safety requirements.

Layered Defense Model

The layered defense model is a layered combination of complementary countermeasures. The number of layers required is dependent on the site configuration but typically includes:

- Outermost perimeter
- Inner perimeter
- Security zone or restricted areas.

The outermost perimeter defines the furthest physical reach controllable by the organization. In rural areas, the perimeter may include fencing, landscaping, and parking areas. Urban environments may be a building or single floor within a shared building.

Inner perimeters are areas found within the outermost perimeter. In a campus situation, a perimeter may be set around every building. In a single building, each floor may have their own inner perimeter.

Security zones are areas within all perimeters that require a higher level of security because of the information or operations being performed.

Considerations

Other departments have concerns related to security. Partnerships can sometimes identify the best approach to ensuring physical security requirements are met and enforced, by:

- Providing the actual security and procedures providing that security
- Addressing the risks ongoing
- Preventing redundant security systems
- Preventing security gaps due to accountability issues.

A defense-in-depth strategy applied to the environment addresses four protection aims:

- Identifying and authenticating individuals requiring access
- Authorization of individuals
- Monitoring and accounting for action within the environment
- Providing a contingency capability in the environment.

Procedural Controls

Procedural controls are designed to manage the perimeters and open areas. They should consist for:

- Guard posts
- Checking and escorting site visitors
- Managing deliveries
- Managing contractor work.

Infrastructure Support Systems

Environmental controls allow sites to comply with health and safety regulations. Security implementations must also comply with these regulations and work in partnership with the environmental controls.

Infrastructure systems to work with include:

- Fire detection and suppression systems
- Perimeter walls, fences, and barriers
- Vehicle and personnel entry and exit gateways.

Entry Points

Entry points are major elements of physical security.

Keys and Locking Systems

Key locks require a physical key to open the lock, while deadbolts have one or more bolts to prevent opening the door. Key systems are required to manage who has a key and to what facilities those keys can be used. Duplication of keys should be managed appropriately.

Combination locks reduce the need for managing physical keys but require additional effort to manage who has knowledge of particular combinations. Keypad and pushbutton locks are similar to combination locks which have a combination of numbers to be learned and secured.

Smart locks are sophisticated mechanisms to reduce access. They can usually be programmed for certain times or specific people.

Walls, Doors and Windows

The design and construction of entry points, such as doors and windows, can provide different levels of security. Sensors used to detect noise or vibrations can be used to identify potential attacks.

Access Controls

The use of card, badge, and pass identifiers provide access controls to physical facilities. More sophisticated access controls include biometric controls.

Electronic Security

Closed-Circuit Television (CCTV) is designed to be a deterrent to attack and monitoring mechanisms to ensure security. An effective CCTV solution requires:

- Positioning cameras at adequate height
- Distribution of cameras to exclude blind spots
- Adequate lighting in all conditions
- Ability to adjust angle and focus remotely
- Ability to record
- Tying camera system to the alarm system
- Regular servicing of movable parts
- Human monitoring and intervention.

Physical Intrusion Detection Systems can offer protection for specific areas. Different technologies for IDS include:

- Electrical circuits
- Light beams
- Passive infrared detector (PIR)
- Microwave and ultrasonic systems.

Remote computing and telecommuting require particular physical and procedural protection for devices, associated media, and information management. These measures include:

- Carrying devices in unmarked bags or briefcases
- Transporting the hard disk separately from the laptop
- Using tamper detective measures, tracing software, or invisible marking systems
- Protecting against illicit access.

Protection and Management Services

Some organizations may contract out for physical security services and therefore should address:

- Contractually binding managed services to meet physical and procedural security requirements
- Ensuring the ability to audit or test provided security services
- Maintaining the communication path between the organization and contracted service.

To test the capabilities of the security measures, audits, drills, and exercises should be performed on a regular basis. Vulnerability and penetration tests allow active attempts to gain unauthorized access to fully test the current implementation.

Lack of regular maintenance and service can lead to potential vulnerabilities in security solutions. Active education and awareness can re-enforce the security requirements of the organization.

Defense in Depth

Defense in Depth is a strategy intended to delay rather than prevent the advance of an attacker. A delay allows time for countermeasures to be applied effectively. Also referred to as elastic defense or deep defense, this strategy is based on military practices where a single, strong defensive line is replaced with a defense line where the attack loses momentum over a period of time or spreads out over a large geographic area. Once this is done, counter attacks are applied to the attacker's weak points.

Implementation of Defense in Depth looks at the physical and logical aspects of access to a system and addresses possible vulnerabilities in personnel, technology, and operations.

Physical Security Implementation

The physical security implementation of defense in depth strategies applies checkpoints of access to facilities and networks. At each checkpoint, the following protections aims are exploited:

- Identifying and authenticating individuals requiring access
- Authorization of individuals
- Monitoring and accounting for action within the environment
- Providing a contingency capability in the environment.

Implementation in Computing

Each of the following is possible layers that can be applied in a defense in depth strategy:

- Authentication and password security
- Antivirus software
- Firewalls
- Demilitarized zones
- Intrusion detection systems
- Packet filters

- Routers and switches
- Proxy servers
- Virtual Private Networks
- Logging and Auditing
- Biometrics
- Timed access control
- Cryptography.

The fundamental principle of cryptography is to take a plaintext message and convert it to ciphertext using a series of substitutions and transpositions.

Crypto Concepts

History of Cryptography

Evidence of cryptography dates back to simple substitution in hieroglyphics in ancient Egypt. The Spartans had a Spartan scytale; the Romans, the Caesar cipher.

In 1466, Leon Battista Alberti had an idea for a cryptographic key. Blais de Vigenere advanced the technology of cryptography by creating an enhanced polyalphabetic cipher.

As modern technology progressed, cryptography became mechanical with the advent of cipherdisks and rotors. The more famous of these machines were the Confederate Army's CipherDisk, The German Enigma machine, and the Japanese Red and Purple machines.

Though the technology has advanced, the concepts and principles of cryptography have not changed.

Purpose of Cryptography

Cryptography has the basic purpose of protecting information from unauthorized access, whether it is being stored or transmitted.

Cryptographic algorithms are used to encrypt information. Encryption ensures that the information can only be read by authorized persons. To be authorized, the person must possess an encryption key. A key is what makes the algorithm work, and can be used to decrypt the message as well.

Data is encrypted on a network using link or end-to-end encryption.

Link encryption will encrypt all the data along the communications path, including the routing information. At each point in the communication path, the data is decrypted and encrypted again as it goes to the next point.

End-to-end encryption is performed at the beginning and end points of a transmission. The routing information is not encrypted to allow the data to be routed properly along the network.

Uses for Cryptography

The security fundamentals of confidentiality, availability, and integrity are supported by cryptography. By altering or hiding a message, cryptography supports the need for confidentiality. Integrity checks which verify whether a message has been altered can be performed by cryptographic tools. Cryptography is used to limit access though passwords, including one-time passwords used within token-based authentication systems.

Nonrepudiation protects an original message from being altered by the recipient and then passed off as the original message. This is done through public key cryptography and digital signatures.

Several methods are used by cryptographic tools to determine the authenticity of the message and the sender, including:

- Hash functions
- Digital signatures
- Message authentication codes (MACs).

Cryptography Methods

Two primary methods are used to encrypt data: stream and block.

Stream-based ciphers are often found in hardware implementations while block-based ciphers are found in software.

Stream-based ciphers are most commonly used in voice and video transmission. The operation mixes the plaintext with a keystream generated by the cryptosystem in an exclusive-or (XOR) process.

Substitution is the primary function of streaming: the substitution of one character or bit for another. Specific rules need to be followed for success stream-based ciphering:

- The strength of the keystream must not be predictable or easily guessed.
- Key management processes must be secure from attack.

Block ciphers focus on blocks of text to encrypt. A message is broken down into a preset size. These sizes typically follow ASCII character sizes of 64, 128, 192, and so on.

Substitution and transposition are used within the operation of a block cipher making it stronger than most stream-based ciphers. They are usually more expensive to implement.

Ciphers

Substitution is the replacing of a character with another character. This is typically done by shifting the alphabet positions.

Transposition, or permutation, relies on transposing or interchanging the order of the letters.

Playfair Cipher

Used by the ally forces in the WWII, the Playfair cipher starts with an agreement of a key word by the sender and receiver. It is a substitution cipher. A table is created using that word and the rest of the alphabet.

A message is separated in groups of two, ignoring the spaces in the message. Repeating letters are grouped with a filler text such as X.

The two letter group defines the parameters of a logical rectangle within the table that was created. The letter grouping is replaced with the letters in the opposite corners of the rectangle. If the letter grouping is on the same row or column, the replacement is done with the next letters in the same row or column respectively.

Transposition Ciphers

The simplest transposition cipher is called a rail fence. The message is written and read on two or more lines by alternating diagonal rows. The final message strings the created rows together. In a rail fence, there is no substitution taking place, just a reordering of the letters.

An early form of cryptography used rectangular substitution tables. In this method, the sender and receiver agreed on the size and structure of the table holding the message, as well as the order for reading the message.

Each letter in the message occupies a space in the table. Depending on the order for reading agreed upon, the final message is a string of rows or columns.

Monoalphabetic and Polyalphabetic Ciphers

The Caesar cipher is a form of monoalphabetic cipher: a simple substitution algorithm crated by shifting the alphabet over three places.

Monoalphabetic ciphers can also utilize a scrambled version of the alphabet. The fundamental principle for these ciphers is that each letter is replaced by another letter consistently throughout the message.

Monoalphabetic ciphers are still driven by the characteristics of plaintext language, making them relatively easy to decipher. Polyalphabetic ciphers are harder to decipher because they use several alphabets for substituting the plaintext.

In a polyalphabetic cipher, each letter is substituted by a letter from a different alphabet. Since the number of alphabets is typically limited, they are recycled as the message proceeds.

Blais de Vigenere developed a polyalphabetic cipher using 26 alphabets and a key word. Each alphabet was offset by one space and grouped in a table. The top row represented the plaintext values, while the first column represents the substitution alphabets.

The sender and receiver agree on a message key which is repeated for the length of the plaintext message. The individual letters of the message and key are cross-referenced on the table to identify the appropriate ciphertext letter.

Modular Mathematics and Running-Key Ciphers

Modular Mathematics starts with matching each letter of the alphabet with its corresponding numerical value. The English alphabet is calculated as mod 26 because it has 26 letters in the alphabet. Each letter in the alphabet is run through the equation:

Ciphertext = plaintext + key (mod 26)

The numerical value of the plaintext letter is added to the numerical value of the key letter. If the sum of the two values is greater than 26, a subtraction is made of 26. The result is the numerical value of the the ciphertext letter.

A running key cipher uses modular mathematics to encrypt the plaintext message. The key is repeated along the length of the message. Each letter is put through the equation using the corresponding key letter until a ciphertext is created.

One-time Pads

These are often referred to as Vernam ciphers because of the work of Gilbert Vernam. He proposed the one-time use of a key. The key must be as long as the plaintext message without any repeats.
A one-time pad uses the principles of modular mathematics by adding the numeric values of the letters and the key. The difference is the random creation of the key.

For one-time pads to work, a cryptographic pad must be used and sent to both the sender and receiver through a secure exchange mechanism.

Other Ciphers

The purpose of steganography focuses on hiding a message rather than encrypting it. Messages can be hidden in an image, digital music, or video.

Watermarking is inserted into a file or document to ensure that the object is not improperly copied or stolen. The mark does not need to be visible.

Cryptography Forms

The two primary forms of cryptography are symmetric and asymmetric

Symmetric Ciphers

Symmetric ciphers utilize an algorithm that operates on a single cryptographic key that is used to encrypt and decrypt the message. This encryption process comes in many names:

- Single key
- Same key
- Shared key
- Secret key
- Private key.

The last two names represent the key factor in using symmetrical algorithms: securing the cryptographic key. The result is extensive focus on key management. This requires not only the generation of the key but also the secure transmission of the key to both the sender and receiver of the message. To ensure security, the key is often sent separate from the message itself, called out-of-band distribution.

Some of the more common symmetric algorithms are:

- Data Encryption Standard (DES)
- Advanced Encryption Standard (AES)
- International Data Encryption Algorithm (IDEA)
- CAST
- Secure and Fast Encryption Routine (SAFER)
- Blowfish
- Twofish
- RC5
- RC4.

Data Encryption Standard

The Data Encryption Standard (DES) became a standard in 1977 when adopted by several US federal government agencies. Today, the encryption is used extensively in many financial, VPN, and online encryption systems.

The origins of DES are based on the work of Harst Feistal using the Lucifer algorithm. The core principle of the algorithm is to take an input block of plaintext and divide it in half. Each half is then put through an XOR operation to alter the other half.

Each DES key is 64 bits in length with each eighth bit ignored, leaving an effective length of 56 bits.

There are five separate modes of DES, including:

- Electronic Codebook Mode (ECB)
- Cipher Block Chaining Mode (CBC)
- Cipher Feedback Mode (CFB)
- Output Feedback Mode (OFB)
- Counter Mode (CTR).

The DES is a block mode cipher, though the last three modes were developed to operate like a stream mode cipher in order to be more versatile and support stream-based applications.

ECB is the most basic mode of DEC. It encrypts each 64-bit block of text independently. It is used for very short messages.

With the CBC, the result of encrypting one block of data is used to encrypt the next block of data.

CFB will segment the input into blocks of 8 bits, or the size of one character. Each bit produced in the keystream is the result of a predetermined number of fixed ciphertext bits. The operation has the ciphertext result of the XOR calculations feed back in a shift register for the keystream.

In OFB mode, the keystream is generated independent of the message. The operation is the same as CFB, except that the encrypted keystream is fed into the shift register to create the next portion of the keystream.

High-speed applications use counter mode. It is named because a 64-bit random data block is used as the first initialization vector. This block is called counter and is different for every block of plaintext. Each subsequent counter is incremented by 1. The counter is encrypted and used as a keystream that is XORed with the plaintext. Since the keystream and the message are separate from each other, several blocks of data can be processed at the same time.

DES is susceptible to brute-force attacks because of the short key used. To overcome this weakness, a stronger version of DES was utilized by running the encryption process twice over the same plaintext message using different keys. This is commonly called a double DES.

Unfortunately, man-in-the-middle attacks are effective against double DES solutions, which led to the design of triple DES. The solution utilizes two encryption keys and three encryption attempts. The plaintext message is encrypted using the first key, then the second, then the first key again.

Another mode of triple DES, EDE2, performs a decryption using the second key. Therefore the process used on the plaintext message is to encrypt using the first key, decrypt with the second key, then encrypt with the first key again. This mode is compliant to ISO 8732 and ANS X9.17.

EEE3 and EDE3 are triple DES modes utilizing three encryption keys.

Advanced Encryption Standard

In 1997, the National Institute of Standards and Technology (NIST) adopted the Advanced Encryption Standard (AES) as a replacement for DES and 3DES. The standard is based on the Rijndael algorithm created by Drs. Joan Daemon and Vincent Rijmen of Belgium. NIST chose AES after considering several possible candidates.

The Rijndael algorithm uses block sizes of 12 8, 192, and 256 bits with keys of the same lengths. The number of operating rounds used is related to the size of the key: 10, 12, and 14 respectively. AES supports only one block size.

To encrypt a plaintext message, the input is placed into a 128-bit state array while the key is placed into a similar table. Then, four major operations are conducted on the message:

- Substitute bytes – an S-box is used to substitute byte-by-byte on the entire block
- Shift rows – each row in the table is offset
- Mix columns – each value in a column is substituted based on the values of the data

- Add round key – each byte is XORed with the key for the current round. Additional rounds are performed with a different key.

Other Encryption Methods

International Data Encryption Algorithm (IDEA) is meant to be a replacement for DES and works off a 128-bit key within a 64-bit operation. Eight rounds of transposition and substitution are performed using modular addition and multiplication and bitwise XOR. IDEA was developed by Xuejai Lai and James Massey in 1991.

Carlisle Adams and Stafford Tavares developed CAST in 1996. A variant, CAST-256, was a candidate for AES and is a Feistal-type block cipher using 128-bit blocks and keys the size of 128, 192, 160, 224, and 256 bits. 48 rounds of encryption are performed on a plaintext message.

Secure and Fast Encryption Routine (SAFER) was developed by James Massey which worked on 64-bit or 128-bit blocks. A variation of SAFER is used for Bluetooth.

Blowfish is a Feistal-type cipher developed by Bruce Schneier. It is an extremely fast cipher that can be implemented in as little as 5K of memory. The cipher divides the input block in half and works on both halves using variable key sizes from 32 to 448 bits on a 64-bit input and output blocks.

One major characteristic of Blowfish is that the S-boxes are created from the key and stored for later use. The processing time required to change keys and recompute the S-boxes make Blowfish unsuitable for applications with limited process power or where keys are changed frequently. Despite this, Blowfish is considered unbreakable.

Twofish is a version of Blowfish developed by a Bruce Schneier and a team of cryptographers to provide another candidate for AES. It performs 16 rounds of encryption using keys of 128, 192, or 256 bits on blocks of 128 bits.

RC5 was developed by Ron Rivest of RSA Data Security. It utilized a key varying from 0 to 2040 bits, with the number of rounds ranging from 0 to 255. The length of the input words could be 16, 32, or 64-bit lengths. It has four modes of operation:

- RC5 – similar to DES ECB
- RC5-CBC – a cipher block chaining mode
- RC5-CBC-Pad – combined chaining with the ability to handle any length of plaintext
- RC5-CTS – called ciphertext stealing.

RC4 was also developed by Ron Rivest in 1987 and became the widely used stream cipher used in WEP and SSL/TLS. A variable key length was used ranging from 8 to 2048 bits. The key initiates a state vector 256 bits in length and will contain all possible values of 8-bit number from 0 to 255. The state is generated into the keystream which is XORed with the plaintext message.

Asymmetric Algorithms

The idea behind asymmetric algorithms was introduced in 1976 by Drs. Whit Diffie and Martin Hellman The idea utilizes two different keys linked mathematically to perform cryptographic operations. Typically, one key is used to encrypt, while the other is used to decrypt.

These concepts were the introduction to public key cryptography. To use an asymmetric algorithm, a person would need to generate a key pair. One half of the key pair would remain secret known only to the key holder, called the private key. The other half of the key pair could be presented to anyone who wanted a copy, called the public key.

Asymmetric algorithms are one-way functions.

Any message that is encrypted with a public key can only be decrypted with the private key of the pair, retaining the confidentiality of the encrypted message. This is because the sender would be encrypting the message with the public key of the receiver.

Any message that is encrypted using the private key of the sender could be opened and read by anyone possessing the corresponding public key.

The process allows the confidentiality of the message to remain intact and retain proof of origin.

RSA

The most widely used form of public key encryption is RSA. Developed by Ron Rivest, Adi Shamir, and Len Adleman in 1978, RSA is based on factoring the product of two large prime numbers.

The formula used is:

$$C = P^{e} \text{ mod n for encryption}$$

$$P = C^{d} \text{ mod n for encryption}$$

To calculate RSA key pairs, two prime numbers are multiplied together:

$$n = pq$$

The public key is {e, n}. The integer e is relatively prime to (n) which is (p-1)(q-1)

The private key is {d,n}. The integer d is calculated using Euclid's algorithm. de=10(n)+1

To attack the RSA algorithm, three major approaches are used:

- Trying all possible private keys
- Factoring the product of two prime numbers
- Measuring the running time if the decryption algorithm.

Diffie-Hellmann Algorithm

A key exchange algorithm used to enable two users to negotiate or exchange a secret symmetric key used for future encryption. It uses discreet logarithms based on finding the primitive root of a prime number.

Private and public keys are still used. The private key is randomly selected and must be less than the prime number. The two hosts would calculate the private key and a public key individually. The public keys would be exchanged and compute a common session key.

Once complete, the two parties could encrypt their data using a symmetric key.

Other Asymmetric Algorithms

The El Gamal algorithm is based on Diffie-Hellmann's work but allows for message confidentiality and digital signature services.

Elliptic Curve Cryptography utilizes a complex branch of discrete logarithms.

Hybrid Cryptography

Using both symmetric and asymmetric cryptography is a hybrid solution. Diffie-Hellmann is really a hybrid solution because it uses asymmetric encryption to send a symmetric key.

Hybrids are used because:

- Symmetric cryptography is the best solution for encrypting large files
- Asymmetric cryptography can handle the initial requirements for communication setup.

Integrity Controls

Message authentication is the primary concern for most electronic transactions. The concerns include questions such as:

- Has the message been modified?
- Is the sender really who they claim to be?
- Was the message received by the right party?

The controls utilized to maintain message integrity include:

- Checksums
- Hash functions
- Message authentication code.

Checksums

Checksums are used with symmetric key cryptography to manage message integrity. Simple error detecting code or frame check sequences are similar implementations.

The checksum is created and attached to the message. Receivers of the message then decrypt the message and create another checksum to check the integrity of the message.

Hash Functions

Hash functions accept input messages of any length and generate a fixed-length output. The result is referred to as hash code or message digest. The hash is generated by using an algorithm, but no secret key is used.

Simple hash functions will break the message down into fixed-size blocks which are then XORed.

MD5 was developed by Ron Rivest at MIT in 1992 and is the most widely used hashing algorithm. A 128-bit message digest is generated. The message is processed in 512-bit blocks and four rounds. Each round consists of 16 steps.

MD4 was developed in 1990 and does only three rounds of processing with fewer mathematical operations. 128-bit output is typically generated.

Secure Hash Algorithm (SHA) were developed by NIST in 1993 and issued as the Federal Information Processing Standard (FIPS) 180. A revised version became SHA-1 in 1995. SHA is based on the MD4 algorithm and SHA-1 is based on MD5. SHA-1 has four rounds of processing with 20 steps in each round.

The University of Wollongong in Australia developed HAVAL, a method that creates variable length output through a variable number of rounds from every 1024-bit input block. The output may be 128,

160, 192, 224, 256 bits and the rounds can range from 3-5.

HAVAL operates 60 % faster than MD5.

The European RACE Integrity Primitives Evaluation project develop0ed the RIPEMD-160 to overcome the vulnerabilities with MD4 and MD5. The algorithm produces a 160-bit output. It performs five paired rounds of 16 steps.

Message Authentication Code (MAC)

Also known as a cryptographic checksum, MACs are small blocks of data created using the secret key and attached to the message. When a message is received, the secret key is used to generate another MAC. The result provides confidence that the message was not changed during the transaction.

A MAC has characteristics such as:

- Smaller than the message generating it
- Given a MAC, to computer the message generating it is impractical
- Given a MAC and the message generating it, finding another message using the same MAC is impractical.

A DES-based MAC is the most common creation method, but slow compared to a hash function. Hash functions do not have secret keys and cannot be used to create a MAC. RFC 2104 provides a hashed MACing system used in IPSec and other secure Internet protocols.

HMAC operations have the cryptographic strength of hashing algorithm with the protection of a secret key.

Digital Signatures

Digital signatures provide accountability for electronic transactions by ensuring that a message truly comes from the person claiming to have sent it. The digital signature usually consists of the data and time of the signature and a third party to verify the signature.

The Digital Signature Standard (DSS) was proposed as FIPS 186 in 1991. Two methods are used to create a signature: RSA and DSS.

The hash version of a message is created. The RSA method encrypts the hash with the private key of the sender. The DSS method uses the Digital Signature Algorithm (DSA) to sign the hash.

Once a digital signature is created, it is appended to the message and sent to the receiver.

Key Management

Key management is a crucial part of any cryptographic implementation. Control is required over:

- Issuance
- Revocation
- Recovery
- Distribution

- History.

Auguste Kerckhoff's Law states: "a cryptosystem should be secure even if everything about the system, except the key, is public knowledge."

The two elements of secured keys are the size and secrecy of the key.

Key Recovery

A lost key is a potential loss of critical data or backups. Key recovery can be done through:

- Common trusted directories
- Registration of cryptographic keys.

Key Distribution

Key Distribution Centers (KDCs) required the creation of two types of keys:

- Master keys – secret keys shared between each user and the KDC
- Session keys – created when needed and lasting for the duration of a communication session.

ANSI X9.17

ANSI X9.17 is a standard developed for financial institutions to transmit securities and monies securely using an electronic medium. The standard's biggest concern is the secrecy of keys and uses a hierarchical approach. At the bottom of the hierarchy are data keys (DKs) used to encrypt and decrypt messages are only valid for a short time.

At the top of the hierarchy are master key-encrypting keys (KKMs). They are distributed manually and have a greater lifespan than DKs. KKMs are used to encrypt the data keys in a two-tier model. In a three-tier model, KKMs are used to encrypt other key-encrypting keys (KKs) which are used to encrypt the data keys.

Public Key Infrastructure (PKI)

Asymmetric cryptography has allowed the use of symmetric cryptography to be more effective. However, public keys are still public and therefore questionable.

To create confidence in the use of public keys, a trusted public directory of keys can be created. Each user must register with the directory service. A secure communication path is created between the user and the directory allowing keys to be changed. The directory can publish and maintain a list of all active keys and delete or revoke keys that are no longer trusted.

To increase the level of trust, public key certificates can be used. Each user has a certificate. These certificates are exchanged directly with other users or through a certificate authority. A certificate sent from a certificate authority will be signed by the digital signature of the certificate authority and be able to be verified by the recipients. Certificate authorities adhere to X.509 standards.

Revoked certificates are maintained by the certificate authority. Expired certificates are not maintained.

If users need to communication with another user registered with a different certificate authority, the two Certificate Authorities perform cross-certification to allow the communication.

Cryptanalysis and Attacks

Cryptanalysis is used to perform attacks to discover and break the encryption methods used. There are several forms of cryptanalysis:

- Ciphertext-only – attempts to gather several pieces of ciphertext and looks for patterns or statistical data
- Known plaintext – access to the cipher-text and the plaintext of the same message are available which are used to find the cryptographic key
- Chosen plaintext – access to the encryption algorithm is available and tested using several plaintext message to determine the key
- Chosen ciphertext – Similar to the plaintext attack using the decryption device or software and ciphertext
- Social engineering – uses coercion, bribery, or befriending people to gain access to systems

- Brute force - attempts all possible keys to decrypt the ciphertext
- Differential power analysis – also called a side channel attack, it measures the exact execution times and power used by the crypto device to determine the length of the key and algorithm used
- Frequency analysis – works with several other attacks and is useful for attacking substitution ciphers because the plaintext language statistics are known
- Birthday attack – based on the proven theory that given enough time and resources two messages using the same hash value can be found
- Dictionary attack – used with password files, it exploits the poor practices of users in creating passwords
- Replay attack – disrupts and damages processing capabilities by sending repeated files to the host
- Factoring attack – focuses on the RSA algorithm by solving the factoring of prime numbers
- Reverse engineering – done by obtaining a used crypto product and performing reverse engineering on the product
- Random number generations – assumes the predictability of the random number generator allowing patterns to be uncovered
- Temporary files – temporary files are used during calculations by cryptosystems and can be accessed if not deleted or overwritten.

Protocols and Standards

Protocols and standards in cryptography include:

- Pretty Good Privacy (PGP)
- Secure/Multipurpose Internet Mail Extension (S/MIME)
- IPSec
- SSL/TLS
- Telecommunications and Network Security.

OSI Model

OSI stands for Open System Interconnection. The OSI Reference Model focuses on network communications. The model consists of seven layers: uppers layers define functionality while lower three layers focus on end-to-end delivery of data.

The seven layers from top to bottom are:

- Application
- Presentation
- Session
- Transport
- Network
- Data link
- Physical.

OSI Layers

The Application Layer provides communication services to

applications, consisting of an interface between the network and the application. Examples of interfaces include:

- Telnet
- HTTP
- FTP
- Internet browsers
- NFS
- SMTP gateways
- SNMP
- X.400 mail
- FTAM.

The Presentation Layer defines data formats and uses encryption and compression. It supports different protocols for text, data, sound, graphics, and images, including:

- ASCII
- EBCDIC
- MIDI
- MPEG
- GIF
- JPEG
- PICT
- TIFF.

The Session Layer defines processes for establishing, controlling, and terminating communication sessions and provides control and management of multiple bidirectional messages. The session layer allows the presentation layer the perception of a seamless stream of incoming data. Essentially, the layer supports a dialog between the presentation layers of two or more systems. Session protocols include:

- RPC
- SQL
- NFS
- NetBios
- AppleTalk ASP
- Decnet SCP.

The Transport Layer performs flow control through buffering, multiplexing, and parallelization. It enables performs error recovery and provides end-to-end services for:

- Segments upper layers
- Establishing connections
- Sending segments
- Ensures reliable data transport
- Management of data stream.

Examples of transport layer protocols:

- TCP
- UDP
- SPX.

The Network Layer defines end-to-end delivery of packets and logical addressing for packet delivery. This is used to provide path determination and packet switching. The network layer uses routing and routed protocols to provide logical addresses. Protocols on this layer can fragment packets into smaller units to accommodate limited media. Routers work on this level. Examples of network layer protocols:

- IP
- IPX
- AppleTalk DDP
- ICMP.

The Data Link Layer is made up of the LLC and MAC sublayers and allows upper layers to work independently of any physical media. Protocols at this layer perform physical hardware addressing, optional flow control, and error notification. Bridges and switches work on this level. Logical Link Control (LLC) provides framing per IEEE standards. MAC sublayers deal with hardware functions and maintain physical addresses. Data Link protocols used include:

- IEEE 802.3/802.2
- HDLC
- Frame Relay
- PPP
- FDDI
- ATM
- IEEE 802.5/802.2

The Physical Layer deals with the physical characteristics of the transmission, allowing signals to be converted to bits for transports.

It communicates with peer layers regarding the activation, maintenance, and deactivation of a circuit. Connectors, pins, electrical currents, encoding, and light modulation work on this level. Physical layer specifications include:

- EIA/TIA-232, V.35
- EIA/TIA-449, V.24
- RJ-45
- Ethernet
- 802.3
- 802.5
- FDDI
- NRZI
- NRZ
- B8ZS.

Working with the OSI Model

During data transmissions between two hosts, the data is processed through each OSI layer. Headers and trailers are placed before and after the data which is given to the next layer. The sending host's software and hardware create these headers and trailers. Each layer has a header and trailer which reside in each data packet that comprises the data flow. As data passes through the layers, the header and trailer for each layer is added or stripped away.

Each layer may interact with the same layer on another computer to implement functions successfully. The data required for these interactions reside in the headers and sometimes trailers.

The Physical Layer provides delivery of a stream of bits across the medium, decoding the incoming signal into a bit stream. The physical layer ensures bit synchronization. Any received binary pattern is placed into a buffer and informs the Data Link Layer when a data frame has been received.

The Data Link Layer delivers data across the link. It examines the frame check sequence (FCS) in the trailer to determine errors which occurred in transmission. When errors occur, the frame is discarded.

The current host will examine the data link address to determine if the data is addressed to it or whether to process the data further. If the data is addressed to the host, the data is handed to the Network Layer software.

The Network Layer ensures end-to-end delivery. It also examines the destination address. If destination address matches host's address, processing continues and the data is sent to the Transport Layer software.

The Transport Layer reorders the incoming data, and performs error recovery when necessary. Within Layer 4, counters are encoded identifying error recovery and acknowledgment information. Data is then given to the Session Layer.

The Session Layer ensures the completion of a series of messages.

The Session header includes fields signifying the sequence of the packet in the stream. The sequence provides the position of the data packet in the flow. When all flows are complete, the data is passed to the Presentation Layer software.

The Presentation Layer defines and manipulates the data format of the data transmission. Its header is typically found only in initialization flow. Data is converted to the proper format as defined by the header. After data formats are converted, the data is passed to the Application Layer software.

The Application Layer processes the final header and examines the data. Its header contains data on agreements for operating parameters and signals the values for all parameters. The header is typically transmitted at application initialization time only.

Network Protocols

Several protocols are used to allow networking within a computing environment. They work together from each of the levels of the TCP/IP Network Model to provide connectivity, communications, and reliability. The most prominent protocols are:

- TCP
- FTP
- UDP
- TCP/IP suite
- DHCP

- TFTP
- DNS
- HTTP
- HTTPS
- ARP
- SIP
- RTP
- SSH
- POP3
- NTP
- IMAP4
- Telnet
- SMTP
- SNMP2
- SNMP3
- ICMP
- IGMP
- TLS.

TCP/IP Suite

Also referred to as the Internet Protocol Suite, the TCP/IP Suite is a set of communication protocols used for the Internet and other network similar in construction. The two most important protocols are Transmission Control Protocol (TCP) and the Internet Protocol (IP). The TCP/IP model consists of four layers: the link layer, the Internet layer, the transport layer, and the application layer.

The suite uses encapsulation to provide an abstraction of protocols and services and identify the various layers of the suite. The TCP/IP layers can be directly mapped to the OSI model.

Transmission Control Protocol (TCP)

The Transmission Control Protocol is a core component of the Internet Protocol Suite, TCP/IP. TCP focuses on the reliable, ordered delivery of bytes from one computer to another program on another computer. E-mail and file transfer are common applications of TCP because of its ability to control segment size, flow control, rate of data exchange, and network congestion.

As mentioned, TCP is part of the larger TCP/IP suite. The Internet Protocol (IP) is designed to exchange pieces of information in the form of packets, which are sequences of bytes combined with a header and body. The header describes the destination of the packet and is used to forward the packet through the network. The body contains the data being transmitted.

When a large amount of data must be sent across the network, the data can be broken up into several pieces and requests that can be handled by IP. TCP can be used to create a single request and handle all the IP details to transmit the data. This process prevents the problems of IP packets becoming lost or delivered out of order. TCP will detect when these problems happen, request retransmission of lost packets, reorder packets, and minimize network congestion.

File Transfer Protocol (FTP)

File Transfer Protocol is a network protocol for exchanging and manipulating files over a TCP/IP based network. FTP is found within client-server architectures and will utilize separate control and data connections between the application on the client and server sides of the connection.

The use of FTP is driven by the desire to:

- Promote sharing of files
- Encourage use of remote computing
- Shield users from variations in file storage systems
- Transfer data reliably and efficiently.

FTP works in two different transport modes to form a control stream that defines the parameters for sending data. In active mode, the FTP client opens and dynamic port to send the FTP server the dynamic port number and waits for a connection. When the data connection is initiated by the server, the client will bind the source port to port 20 on the FTP server. In passive mode, the FTP server will open a dynamic port and send the FTP client the server's IP address to connect to and the port which the server is listening. When the client makes the connection, it binds the source port to the dynamic port. Extended passive mode works just like passive mode, but only the port number is transmitted.

While data is being transferred through a data stream, the control stream sits idle which can cause problems with timing out with large data transfers across the firewall.

Trivial File Transfer Protocol (TFTP)

The Trivial File Transfer Protocol is a simpler version of FTP that can be implemented with very little memory. It is an excellent tool for transmitting small amounts of data between network hosts, specifically thin clients and IP phones. TFTP is also used to load a basic kernel that will later perform the action installation of a program.

TFTP utilizes UDP and supplies its own transport and session support. The UDP port 69 is its transport protocol. Its primary purpose is to read files from remote servers and write files to remote servers. Unfortunately, its lack of security makes it vulnerable in open Internet sessions and therefore typically restricted to use in private, local networks. Unlike its FTP counterpart, TFTP cannot list directory contents and has no mechanisms for authentication or encryption.

User Datagram Protocol (UDP)

User Datagram Protocol is part of the Internet Protocol Suite. With UDP, computer applications will send messages in the form of datagrams to other hosts on an IP network. Special transmission channels or data paths are not required to send communication.

Also called the Universal Datagram Protocol, UDP uses a simple transmission model without the handshakes required for guaranteeing reliability, ordering, or data integrity. Error checking is assumed to be performed at the application level and ignored by UDP. UDP is popular with time-sensitive data transmissions that can be delayed with error checking processes or to answer small queries from large numbers of clients that exist in packet broadcasting or multicasting. Several common network applications use UDP, such as DNS, IPTV, VoIP, TFTP and online games.

Datagram sockets are used to establish host-to-host communications by UDP applications. These sockets bind the application to service ports that act as endpoints for the data transmission. The packet of the UDP is structures with a header and body, or payload. Application multiplexing and integrity verification of the entire packet is provided, but reliability in the transmission is provided by the application. The UDP header consists of the source port, destination port, length, and checksum.

Dynamic Host Configuration Protocol (DHCP)

The Dynamic Host Configuration Protocol focuses on obtaining configuration information for device operation within an IP network. Used by network applications, DHCP reduces the administration workload and allows devices to be added to the network with little or no manual intervention.

Network parameters assignments to network devices can be automated through one or more DHCP servers. Clients configured for DHCP will send a broadcast query when connecting to the network requesting necessary information from a DHCP server. These servers manage pools of IP addresses and information about configuration parameters used by clients about default gateways, domain names, DNS servers, and other network specific information, The server will receive the broadcasted request from the client and assign an IP address, a lease defining the time length for the IP address and other IP configuration parameters, including the gateway and subnet mask. Allocation of IP addresses is done using one of three methods:

- Dynamic allocation – a range of IP addresses assigned to DHCP and each client computer on the network is configured to request an IP address.
- Automatic allocation – a free IP address is permanently assigned to a request client by the DHCP server from a range defined by the administrator. The DHCP server maintains a table of past IP address assignments to ensure that the same IP address be assigned to the same client.
- Static Allocation – IP addresses are allocated by the DHCP server based on a table with pairs of MAC addresses and IP addresses which are manually completed. Only clients with a MAC address listed in the table can request and be allocated an IP address.

Domain Name System (DNS)

The Domain Name System is a hierarchical naming system for computers, services and other resources connected to a network, namely the Internet of private network. The protocol is used to translate domain names to numerical identifiers (IP addresses) associated with networking equipment. This allows devices connected to the network to be located and addressed.

A domain name space is constructed like a tree of domain names. The tree is divided into zones starting with the root zone. Each DNS zone is a collection of connected nodes served by an authoritative nameserver. Responsibility over any zone can be divided and delegated into smaller zones, or domains.

Domain names are constructed in two or more parts. The rightmost label is the top-level domains, typically represented by a three character universally recognized label that identifies the type of domain devices. The most common labels are:

- .gov US Government entities
- .edu Post Secondary Educational organizations
- .com Commercial organizations
- .mil US Military
- .org Generic label (Miscellaneous)
- .net Network Infrastructures.

The top level domains can be further represented by country specific codes utilizing the two character domains established by ISO 3166.

Domain names also include subdomains and hostnames that are associated to specific IP addresses.

Hypertext Transfer Protocol (HTTP)

Hypertext Transfer Protocol is an application-level protocol used to retrieve inter-linked resources allowing distribution and collaboration. HTTP uses a request and response system to operate. The client is an application or computer used by a user which requests information from a website hosted by a server. The server stores and creates resources which are accessible by HTTP. The protocol runs on top of other protocols, such as TCP. Resources are identified using Uniform Resource Identifiers (URIs) and Uniform Resource Locators (URLs).

When an HTTP client initiates a request with a web server, it establishes a TCP connection through a port, usually port 80. A series of network request and response transactions are performed. The protocol defines eight methods that can be performed on a resource, including:

- HEAD – asks for an identical response to a Get response without a response body
- GET – requests a representation of the resource
- POST – submits data to be processed to the resource
- PUT – uploads a representation of the resource
- DELETE – deletes the resource
- TRACE – allows changes from intermediate servers to be seen by echoing back the received request
- OPTIONS – informs of the HTTP methods supported by the server for the specific URL and allows a functionality check of the web server
- CONNECT – converts the request connection to a

transparent TCP/IP tunnel.

Hypertext Transfer Protocol Secure (HTTPS)

Hypertext Transfer Protocol Secure is a combination of HTTP and the SSL/TLS protocol to enable encryption and secure identification of the server. Used extensively for payment transactions over the Web and other sensitive transactions, HTTPS is based on major certificate authorities installed in browser software. A HTTPS connection is considered secure and trusted if and only if:

- The user trusts the certificate authority to vouch for legitimate websites
- The website can provide a valid certificate signed by a trusted authority
- The certificate correctly identifies the website
- The intervening hops between client and website are trustworthy.

Transport Layer Security (TLS)

Transport Layer Security is a cryptographic protocol which provides security for communications over the network by encrypting segments of the connection at the Transport layer. TLS is based on the Secure Sockets Layer (SSL) and is used in applications for web browsing, electronic mail, Internet faxing, instant messaging and VoIP.

TLS is designed to prevent eavesdropping, tampering, and message forgery of Internet communications by providing endpoint authentication and communications confidentiality. TLS supports unilateral and bilateral authentication and involves three basic phases:

- Peer negotiation
- Key exchange and authentication
- Symmetric cipher encryption and message authentication.

Different encryption algorithms can be used but must be agreed upon by both endpoints within a communication session.

TLS is used in conjunction with HTTP, FTP, and SMTP, tunning on top of them. It can be used with TCP or UDP. It is also used to create a Virtual Private Network by tunneling an entire network stack. SIP uses TLS to protect its application signaling.

Session Initiation Protocol (SIP)

Session Initiation Protocol is a signaling protocol used to control multimedia communication sessions over IP, such as voice and video calls. SIP will enable the creation, modification, and termination of two-party or multiparty sessions comprising of one or more media streams.

SIP utilizes several design elements to HTTP and STMP. It is a TCP/IP based application layer protocol that can run on top of TCP or UDP. Though SIP can work with several other protocols, it is only involved in the signaling portion of a communication session and used to construct and deconstruct voice or video calls. SIP applications utilize another application protocol, RTP, to carry voice and video stream data. It supports the call processing functions and features found in public switched telephone network (PSTN) and operates similar to familiar telephone operation.

Real-Time Transport Protocol (RTP)

The Real-Time Transport Protocol (RTP) defines the standardized packet format for delivering audio and video over the Internet. It is used in communication and entertainment systems involved with streaming media, such as telephony and video conferencing applications. RTP is designed to provide end-to-end, real-time, transfer of multimedia data.

The RTP specification describes two sub-protocols:

- Data Transfer Protocol – deals with the transfer of real-time multimedia data and includes enabled timestamps, sequence numbers, and payload format
- Real time control protocol (RTCP) – specifies QoS feedback and synchronization between media streams.

For each multimedia stream, an RTP session is established consisting of an IP address with ports for both RTP and RTCP.

Simple Mail Transport Protocol (SMTP)

Simple Mail Transport Protocol is an Internet standard for electronic mail. Electronic mail servers and mail transfer units use SMTP to send and receive mail messages, but client mail application use SMTP for sending messages to a mail server. To receive messages, client application use POP or IMAP.

SMTP defines the transport of the message, not the content of the message. Using SMTP, e-mail is submitted from a message user agent (MUA), or the client's email application, to a mail server agent (MSA). The MSA will deliver the mail to a message transfer agent (MTA) which typically resides on the same mail server. SMTP uses port 587 to submit to MSAs and port 25 to transfer to MTAs. The MTA will search the DNS for destination mail exchanger records and relay the mail to the server. Once accepted the MTA will deliver the incoming message using a mail delivery agent (MDA) to the server designated for local mail delivery. The MDA will either store the mail or forward it over a network. An authenticated MUA is used to retrieve mail from the local mail server using PO or IMAP.

Post Office Protocol (POP3)

Post Office Protocol is an application-layer Internet standard which retrieves e-mail from a remote server over a TCP/IP connection. Several versions have been developed and POP3 is the current standard. The use of POP is typically associated with e-mail clients connecting to mail servers, retrieving all messages, storing those messages on the user's computer as new messages, deleting the messages from the server, and disconnecting from the mail server. Some clients have the option to continue storing messages on the server and synchronizing with the client using the POP3 Unique

Identification Listing (UIDL) command.

Internet Message Access Protocol (IMAP)

The Internet Message Access Protocol (IMAP) is another application-layer message retrieval protocol. Unlike POP, IMAP supports both on-line and off-line modes of operations. Messages are generally left on the server until they are explicitly deleted. This allows multiple clients to access the same mailbox.

Most e-mail applications will support either POP or IMAP; however few Internet Service Providers (ISPs) support IMAP.

Telnet

Telnet is used to facilitate bidirectional interactive communications. Access to a command-line interface is provided. This interface is located on a remote host through a virtual terminal connection. Telnet works on TCP.

A connection to TCP port 23 is established by the protocol to a listening Telnet server application. The protocol does not encrypt any data and offers no authentication. These weaknesses have been the primary reasons for the decline in using Telnet; however, it is still used in diagnosing problems without using specialized client software. It can be used to debug network services for SMTP, IRC, HTTP, FTP, and POP.

Secure Shell (SSH)

A more secure protocol with the same functionality of Telnet, Secure Shell allows data to be exchanged using a secure channel between two networked devices. SSH is primarily used on Linux and Unix systems to access shell accounts. Public-key cryptography is used to authenticate remote systems. Often used to log into remote systems and execute commands, SSH will support tunneling, forwarding TCP ports and X11 connections.

SSH-2 has three well-separated layers:

- Transport layer – handles initial key exchange and server authentication and establishes encryption, compression, and integrity verification.
- User Authentication layer -handles client authentication and several methods for authentication including password, public key, and keyboard-interactive.
- Connection layer – defines channels, channel requests, and global requests using SSH services.

Simple Network Management Protocol (SNMP)

Simple Network Management Protocol is a UDP-based network protocol used to monitor network-attached devices for conditions requiring the attention of the network administrator. It is a component of the IP Suite and contains a set of standards for network management, consisting of an application layer protocol, a database schema, and a set of data objects.

When using SNMP, one or more administrative computers monitor or manage a group of hosts on the computer network. These managing systems are referred to as “Masters.” The systems that are being managed are referred to as “Slaves” and will execute an agent that reports information through SNMP to the Masters.

The management data reported by the SNMP agents are viewed as variables and consist of such measures as free memory, system name, and number of running processes. These variables are organized in hierarchies that are described by Management Information Bases (MIBs).

Network Time Protocol (NTP)

Network Time Protocol is used to synchronize the clocks of computer systems over packet-switched, variable-latency data networks. Using UDP port 123, NTP is one of the oldest Internet protocols. It uses a hierarchical, layered system of clock sources. Each level of the hierarchy is referred to as a stratum and assigned a layer number. Each stratum will define its distance from the reference clock and will prevent cyclical dependencies. The different levels are:

- Stratum 0 – consists of atomic clocks, GPS clocks, or radio clocks that are directly connected to the local computer and not the network
- Stratum 1 – computers attached to Stratum 0 devices which typically act as servers for timing requests from other levels. Often called time servers
- Stratum 2 – consists of computers which send NTP

requests to Stratum 1 servers

- Stratum 3 – consists of computers which send NTP requests to Stratum 2 computers.

Internet Control Message Protocol (ICMP)

The Internet Control Message Protocol is used by operating systems on networked systems to send error messages. IP is used to perform the tasks of ICMP making the protocol an integral part of the IP. ICMP messages are a result of errors in IP datagrams and constructed at the Internet layer. The message usually uses the IP datagram with the ICMP response. IP will encapsulate the message with a new IP header and transmit back to the original sending host. The traceroute command and ping utility uses ICMP messaging to function.

Internet Group Management Protocol (IGMP)

The Internet Group Management Protocol is used by IP hosts and adjacent routers to establish memberships to multicast groups. As a communication protocol, it is used by client computers to connect to a local multicast router. Protocol Independent Multicast (PIM) is used to direct multicast traffic from the server to the clients.

Address Resolution Protocol (ARP)

The Address Resolution Protocol aids in determining a host's link layer or hardware address when only its IP address or Network Layer address is known. This is important for local area networking or routing internetworking traffic based on IP addresses when the next hop must be determined. Used in IPv4 networks (IPv6 uses the Neighbor Discovery Protocol (NDP), ARP is a request and response protocol that operates only across the local link that a host is connected to.

Network Devices

Repeater

Repeaters connect different segments of the network by receiving incoming frames, regenerating the preamble, amplifying the signals, and sending the frame out all interfaces. They operate at the physical layer of the OSI.

Repeaters are not aware of packets or frame formats, so they cannot control broadcasts or collision domains. They are also not aware of upper-layer protocols.

The general rule for using repeaters is the 5-4-3 Rule. The rule states that the maximum path between two stations cannot exceed 5 segments with 4 repeaters between those segments and no more than 3 segments populated. A small amount of latency is introduced when using repeaters requiring a transmitting device to take into account the delay introduced in order to detect a collision with another device.

Hub

Hubs work on the physical layer of the OSI model. They perform the same function as repeaters, but through multiple ports. Hubs are typically found in wiring closets to concentrate Thinnet and 10BaseT networks. They are often used within the star topology to facilitate communication between network nodes. There are three types of hubs:

- Passive – does not require an external power source, does not regenerate the signal, and should be considered as part of the cable in respect to cable length
- Active – requires an external power source to allow for regeneration of the signal
- Intelligent – An active hub that provides error detection.

Modem

Modems are used to convert analog to digital and vice versa. For the most part, modem use is an alternative when a wireless hotspot is unavailable but a telephone line is. Connectivity is performed through a dial-up application to a predefined phone number of the service provider which allows connection to the WAN. From there, the user typically has connectivity to the Internet or with the proper credentials, within their companies Intranet. Most homes and small offices have cable modems or ADSL modems that act as hotspots to provide wireless and wired Internet connectivity. To access these modems from the computer, configuration is similar to setting up a Local Area Network using Ethernet.

Network Interface Card

A Network Interface Card, also called the Network interface Controller, is a hardware device to provide an interface between a computer network and devices to allow for a network-capable device to access that network. The NIC has a ROM chip that contains a unique MAC address which allows the device to be identified on the LAN. The NIC exists on Layer 1 and 3 of the OSI model.

A NIC uses one or more techniques to transfer data:

- Polling – the status of peripherals under program control are examined by the NIC
- Programmed I/O – a designated peripheral is alerted by having a MAC address being applied to the system's address bus
- Interrupt-driven I/O – the peripheral alerts the NIC when its ready to transfer data
- Direct Memory Access (DMA) – an intelligent peripheral assumes control of the system bus to access memory directly.

Media Converter

Media Converters allow network traffic to be passed between different types of network ports. Generally this is found between twisted pair and fiber optic solutions. They can support different data communication protocols and cabling types.

One can find media converters as small standalone devices or as PC card converters. High port-density chassis systems are available.

Bridge

Bridges, like repeaters, connect different segments of a network. They are also protocol transparent. Unlike repeaters, bridges are intelligent devices working on the data link layer of the OSI model.

Bridges can control the collision domains on the network. They will filter any incoming frames with the destination MAC addresses that are on the same segment where the frame arrived from, preventing the frame from being forwarded. Bridges can do this because they have already learned the MAC layer address for each node on each segment and the interface they are located on. If the address is unknown, the bridge will forward the frame in a process called flooding, which is also used in broadcast frames.

Bridges store the entire frame until the CRC is verified and forward the frame, if a CRC error is detected, the frame is discarded. The Spanning-Tree Protocol is implemented to build a loop free network topology. With the protocol, different bridges communicate with each other, exchanging information such as priority and bridge interface MAC addresses. As a group, they select a root bridge and implement the protocol which places some interfaces into a hold state while others are in a forward mode, resulting in a single path to send the frame.

Switch

Switches are more advanced than bridges. They use fast integrated circuits to reduce latency normally introduced by bridges. They generally have more ports than bridges and run faster. They store MAC addresses for each part and implement the Spanning-Tree Protocol. Where they differ from bridges is that each part is a separate collision domain, but all are part of the broadcast domain. Broadcasts are not controlled by switches.

Switches can run in cut-through mode which allows a frame to be forwarded before the entire frame enters the buffer. Unfortunately, cut-through operations increase the probability that error frames are propagated on the network and most switches perform store-and forward operations.

Wireless Access Point

Access points provide an entry point into the wireless network. The hardware is half duplex with an intelligence equivalent to a sophisticated Ethernet switch. Access points have the ability to communicate with the client, the network and other access points.

An access point can be configured in three modes:

- Root mode
- Repeater mode
- Bridge mode.

Root mode is typically the default configuration. It is used when connecting the access point to a wired network backbone through a wired interface. Root-based access points are typically Ethernet driven. When multiple access points are connected to the same wired network distribution, they are in communication with each other's coordinating roaming functions.

Bridge mode connects two or more wired networks using wireless access points.

Repeater mode provides a wireless upstream link to a wired link. A client will connect to an access point in repeater mode. A wireless connection from the repeater is made with a root access point upstream.

Use of repeater access points is not recommended because:

- Cells around each access point must overlap by more than 50%, reducing the range available to clients
- Throughput is reduced since the repeater is communicating with the upstream access points and all clients
- Users attached to repeaters typically experience low throughput and high latency.

Access points can be portals allowing client connectivity from wireless 802.11 networks to wired 812.3 or 802.5 networks. Several hardware and software options are available, including:

- Fixed or detachable antennas

- Advanced filtering capabilities
- Removable (modular) radio cards
- Variable output power
- Varied types of wired connectivity.

Devices with detachable antennas allow connection to any antenna with any length of cable required. Some access points are shipped with diversity antennas which allow the use of multiple antennas with multiple inputs on a single receiver.

An access point may include MAC or protocol filtering capabilities which is used to prevent intruder access to the wireless LAN. Access points can be configured to filter devices that are not listed in the MAC filter list in the administrative controls of the access point device. Protocol filtering controls what protocols can be used on a wireless link.

Some access points have the ability to add special functionality by providing PCMCIA slots. This allows additional radios to be added or removed from the device. With two PCMCIA slots, a device can have one radio card to become an access point while another radio card can act as a bridge or as independent access points, increasing the number of users that can connect.

The administrator can control the power used by the access point to send data through variable power output functions. Controlling powers allow the range of the access point to be controlled. The more power used, the greater the distance available to access the wireless network.

Fixed output access points are alternatives. Changes to power can be made using:

- Amplifiers
- Attenuators
- Long cables
- High-gain antennas.

Access points can link to most network types. Understanding the limitations of wired connections to the access point from the core network follows because network restrictions.

Configuring and managing access points are dependent on the feature set by the manufacturer. Most devices include at least a console, telnet, USB, or built-in web server. Some models may include custom configuration management software. An access point is typically preconfigured with an IP address. A hardware reset button is available to reset the device to factory defaults.

Several additional features are available. The more features available, the greater the expense for the device. Some of the features available on Small Office, Home Office (SOHO) devices and Enterprise devices include:

SOHO devices

- MAC filtering

- WEP (64-bit or 128-bit)
- USB or console configuration interfacing
- Built-in web server configuration interface (simple)
- Custom configuration applications (simple).

Enterprise

- Custom configuration applications (advanced)
- Built-in web server configuration interface (advanced)
- Telnet access
- SNMP management
- 802.1x/EAP
- RADIUS client
- VPN client and server
- Static or dynamic routing
- Repeater functions
- Bridging functions.

Functionality support can vary drastically within the same feature; some devices partially support the feature while others fully support it.

Router

Routers make forwarding decisions based on network layer addressing. They control collision domains and broadcast domains. Each interface of a router is considered a different broadcast domain which is defined by the subnet and mask. Routers are protocol aware and are capable of forwarding or limiting packets of routed protocols.

When forwarding packets between networks of different media, routers are the preferred method. Additionally, they have methods to filter traffic, provide route redundancy, load balancing, hierarchical addressing, and multicast routing.

Firewall

Firewalls are devices designed to prevent unauthorized access and can be implemented using hardware or software. All packets going through the firewall are examined using a set of predefined rules.

The types of firewalls include:

- Packet Filter – the most common type of firewall placed between a trusted and untested network
- Application Proxy – inspects all packets at the application layer to filter any specific commands
- Stateful Inspection – monitors packets for the purpose of filtering but also monitors the status of connections
- Screened Host – uses a packet filter firewall and application proxy (Bastion) host
- Screened Subnet – uses two packet filter firewalls and a bastion host.

Specialized Network Devices

Multilayer Switch

A multilayer switch (MLS) is a networking device that acts like a layer

2 switch, but provides additional functions on higher OSI layers.

At layer 3, a MLS can use application -specific integrated circuit (ASIC) hardware to perform packet switching operations normally attributed to routers. Routers perform this function using a microprocessor. A MLS will route between VLAN and ports.

A special version of MLS, the 4-7 switch will use packet information up to the seventh layer of the OSI model. Also called content switches, content services switches, web switches, or application switches, 4-7 switches are typically used for load balancing between groups of servers. It uses NAT to ensure that the load balancing is transparent to the customer. To reduce loads on the servers receiving the traffic, they can also perform standard operations normally performed by the server.

Load Balancer

Many routers perform the function of load balancing, which is a technique for distributing workload across two or more computers or network resources. This provides optimal resource utilization, maximum throughput, minimizes response time, and avoids overload.

Multiple components enabled with load balancing can increase the reliability of the network through redundancy.

DNS Server

DNS Server is an application or server which implements a name-server protocol, specifically the Domain Name System (DNS). The DNS maintains the domain namespace and provides translation services between namespaces.

Authoritative name servers provide original, definitive answers to DNS queries. They can be master or slave servers. A master server will store the original copies of all zone records, while the slave server uses an automated updating mechanism to maintain a copy of master records. Every domain name is assigned a set of authoritative name servers, specifically the assignment of primary and secondary name servers.

To improve efficiency and reduce the DNS traffic over the Internet, DNS cache servers may be utilized. These servers store DNS query results for a period of time for a particular domain name record.

Traffic Shaper

Traffic shaping is a technique used to optimize or guarantee performance, lower latency and increase usable bandwidth. This is done by delaying packets that meet specific criteria. Bandwidth throttling aims to control the volume of traffic being sent into the network for a specific period of time. Rate limiting controls the maximum rate which traffic is sent. Traffic shaping typically performs at the outer edges of the network to control the traffic entering.

Also called a bandwidth shaper, a traffic shaper will delay packets based on three classifications of traffic:

- Sensitive traffic – packets that are expected to arrive on time and must be guaranteed to travel through the network without delay. For this reason, traffic shaping is not applied to this class of traffic or is prioritized over other classes. VoIP, online gaming, video conferencing, and web browsing are examples of sensitive traffic
- Best-Effort Traffic – this form of traffic is deemed non-detrimental and can be delayed. They are not sensitive to Quality of Service metrics. Peer-to-peer applications and email are examples of this form of traffic
- Undesired traffic – identifies spam or malicious attacks which is typically identified and blocked completely.

Proxy Server

Proxy servers are used in networking environments to act as an intermediary between clients seeking resources and other servers. When a client connects to the proxy server, it requests a service or other resources which is available from a different server. The proxy server serves four purposes:

- To allow servers behind it to remain anonymous
- To provide caching services to allow faster access to resources
- To censor network services and content
- To forge transmitted content before delivery.

If a proxy server passes requests and responses unmodified, it is considered a tunneling proxy or gateway. Proxy servers can perform one or more additional functions:

- Caching Proxy – speeds up service requests by retrieving content saved from previous requests
- Web Proxy – focuses on WWW traffic in order to cache
- Content-filtering Web Proxy – provides administrative control over content
- Hostile Proxy – eavesdrops on dataflow between client machines and the web
- Intercepting Proxy – a proxy server with functions of a gateway or router
- Forced Proxy – filters all traffic and forces the user to configure a proxy
- Suffix Proxy – allows access to web content by appending the name of the process server to the URL
- Reverse Proxy – Provides encryption/SSL acceleration, load balancing, compression, and traffic control to several web servers receiving Internet traffic
- Tunneling Proxy – used to move through implemented blocking policies.

Channel Service Unit (CSU)/ Data Service Unit (DSU)

A Channel Service Unit is a bridging device for T-carrier lines that is used for several purposes including:

- Performing loopback testing

- Performing bit stuffing
- Providing compatible framing and formatting patterns
- Preventing electrical interference
- Regenerating Points before signal reaches multiplier or DTE.

CSUs are required by PSTM providers for digital interfaces that terminate in a DSU.

Data Service Unit is a circuit terminating equipment to transform digital data between the telephone service provider and local equipment. It converts bipolar digital data from a CSU into a format usable by a DTE. DSUs have two or more ports: one port is the WAN port, another is the DTE port.

Routing Fundamentals

Interior versus Exterior Gateway Protocols

In Internet terms, an autonomous system (AS) is a set of connected IP routing prefixes under the control of one or more network operators which adhere to a clearly defined policy. A single organization could have more than one AS, but the Internet only recognizes the routing policy of the organization.

The network infrastructure of an organization can consist of several segments. The most basic structure is the internal network, often referred to as the Intranet, and the external network, or Internet.

However, many organizations have developed an intermediary network structure between the internal and external networks called an Extranet that allows access to organizational resources without exposing too much of the organization's assets.

But even within the internal network, the infrastructure may be divided into physical or logical autonomous systems, or segments or domains. While one of the key purposes of these segments is to allow the connected users within them to function as intended across the network with each other, connecting the different segments together is also desirable. However, the rules or policies governing connecting internal segments are typically much different than the rules and policies governing connecting internal segments with external segments.

To manage and enforce these rules and policies, specialized routers, or gateways are placed at the adjoining borders of each segment. To manage the rules for connecting between internal segments, these routers are provided Interior Gateway Protocols (IGP). The routers connecting internal and external resources are provided Exterior Gateway Protocols. These protocols manage the network traffic in both directions; though in some implementations one router may manage traffic being sent from a particular network segment while another router manages the traffic received.

Static and Dynamic Routing

Static routing is the process of the network administrator manually entering routing entries on the router. The entries within the table do not change until the administrator changes them. Static routing is useful for hub-and-spoke topologies with low bandwidth as no routing protocol traffic will be generated by the router.

Dynamic routing, however, uses routing protocols to build tables from information received from other routers in the internetwork. If a change occurs on the network, the best routes are recalculated by the set of routers.

There are two types of dynamic routing protocols:

- Distance vector
- Link state.

Network Hop

When a host on the network sends a data packet to a particular destination, the packet itself may have to go through one or more routers before the destination is reached. Each instance that a packet is moved on to another router is considered a hop.

The distance between two hosts is measured in hops. The hop count is a logical, not physical, measurement of distance. Two computers sitting physically close may be on the same network segment and have a hop count of 0, or be on different network segments and have a hop count of 3 or 4.

The Internet Protocol will specify a limit for the number of hops that a packet is allowed, called the Hop Limit. If the packet exceeds the hop limit, it will be discarded. This is useful to prevent infinite loops by a packet that cannot find its destination.

The 'next hop' refers to the next router, or gateway, that the packet will be forwarded to in order to reach its destination.

Routing tables contain the IP address of the destination network and the IP address of the next router to the network destination. When the routing table stores the next hop for all 'known' destinations, the activity is called next-hop forwarding. In these cases, each router knows only one step, the next, of the path required by the packet.

Routing Tables

Routing provides a relay system where packets are forwarded from one device to the next. For this system to work, routers must be able to interpret the logical topology of the network. Several logical addresses schemes can be known to routers and information is constantly exchanged to keep each router current on the topology being used.

Routing tables are database repositories populated with each possible logical destination network known to the router. Entries in the tables are usually listed in ascending order for major networks, descending order for subnetworks. Routing tables can be updated manually (static) or dynamically.
A routing table entry will point to an IP address, which the router uses to find an interface to and switches the packet into an outbound

interfaces buffer. The router will also map the Layer 2 address and the Layer 3 address. The packet will be encapsulated into a layer 2 frame appropriate for the outbound interface, which will forward the packet to the next device. This is done at each router until the packet reaches its destination.

Statically defined entries are manually entered into the router and consist of entering individual configuration commands to define specific routes to routers. A router will only be able to forward packets to subnets in its routing table. However, routers always knows about directly connected routes. Static routes allow the router to forward packets to subnets not attached to it.

With dynamic routing, a routing protocol identifies the best path within a network and works to maintain the route. If the route fails, the routing protocol finds another one. Easier to use than static routes, dynamic routes utilize more CPU cycles and network bandwidth.

Updates to the routing table can occur using the distance vector and link-state protocols. Distance vector protocols use a routine, periodic broadcast that contains the entire routing table. The broadcast will only go as far as the next hop but allows a router to see the network from the perspective of its neighbors. Distance is added using the router's metric and the neighbor's metric.

Link-state protocols use a triggered-update type of broadcast generated when a topology change occurs. The broadcasts contain information about the change and are flooded to all devices.

Bandwidth is saved since less information is contained in the broadcast packet. Sometimes, a periodic broadcast is required to verify the network topology.

Convergence

Convergence is a concept typically attributed to dynamic routing. The concept refers to a set of routers collecting all available topology information from each other from the implemented routing protocol. If the information gathered does not conflict in any way, it is assumed the real state of the network is reflected and the routers are considered converged.

When a routing protocol is enabled, the routers on the network will attempt to exchange information about the network topology. The routing protocol determines what information is exchanged. Once all the information has been distributed to all participating routers in the process, a state of convergence has been achieved. Any changes to the network that affect the routing table will temporarily disrupt the convergence.

The amount of time that the convergence state is disrupted is based on the size of the network and the type of routing protocols used. Larger networks will take longer to converge than smaller networks. RIP is a slow converging protocol, while OSPF is a fast converging routing protocol. Additionally, certain configurations and hardware conditions may prevent convergence.

Routing Protocols

Distance Vector

Distance vector protocols advertise routes based on vectors of distance and direction. Distance is measured in router hop count and direction is the next hop router to forward the packet. With distance vector, each router is asked to send all or part of its routing table to neighboring routers. The sent routing table is added to the existing routing table of the neighboring router and then sent on to its neighbors. The table is sent periodically to ensure changes to the network are updated in the routing table.

Distance vector protocols include:

- IP Routing Information Protocol (RIP)
- Interior Gateway Routing Protocol (IGRP)
- IPX Routing Information Protocol (IPX RIP)
- AppleTalk Router Table Maintenance Protocol (RTMP)
- DEC DNA Phase IV
- XNS Routing Information Protocol (XNS RIP).

Routing Information Protocol (RIP) is a distance vector protocol and uses hop counts as a metric. The maximum hop count is 15 indicating that a packet can be sent through a maximum of 15 devices including the destination.

RIP is a classful protocol which does not support VLSM or authentication and is designed for smaller networks. It is typically found in UNIX environments. Updates are sent to neighboring routers every 30 seconds. An expiration timer, 180 seconds, is implemented to set a route as invalid. Another timer, 240 seconds, is set to remove a route from the routing table. Cisco implements an additional hold-down timer, 180 seconds, for changes on a route which prevents any additional changes from being accepted until the timer expires.

Algorithms are employed by RIP to prevent routing loops, which include triggered updates and split horizon with poison reverse. Triggered updates are routing table updates sent before the update timer has expired, sending updates to the routing table before the 30 second interval. A triggered update usually indicates a metric change for a particular route.

Split horizon is a technique where the route learned from a neighboring router is not sent back to the neighboring router. Poison reverse will send the route information with a metric of unreachable instead of suppressing the route.

RIPv2 has the same distance vector characteristics as RIP, but includes support for VLSM, authentication of route updates and multicast updates.

Developed by Cisco, Interior Gateway Routing Protocol (IGRP) is meant to overcome limitations with RIP. Hops are not used as a metric like RIP and IGRP will track up to 255 hops. Updates are still made periodically with neighboring routers. It is classful and implements split horizon, triggered updates, and hold-down timers. It cannot implement VLSM, but will load balance over unequal cost links.

The IGRP update timer is set at 90 seconds, the Invalid timer is 270 seconds. The flush timer is 630 seconds. Triggered updates will initiate the hold down timer of 280 seconds.

Instead of using hops as a metric, IGRP uses a composite of bandwidth, delay, load, and reliability. The maximum transmission unit (MTU) is tracked but not used in the metric calculation.

Border Gateway Protocol (BGP) is an IP Exterior Gateway Protocol (EGP) which connects different autonomous systems and typically connects larger organizations to the Internet. The protocol performs routing among multiple autonomous systems or domains. With other BGP systems, its reachability information is exchanged. Within an autonomous system, all other routing protocols are used as Interior Gateway Protocols (IGP).

IPX RIP is a distance vector routing protocol for Novell which sends periodic updates every 60 seconds. A tick is used as a metric, which is a delay assigned to interfaces off the router of 1.18th of a second. When two paths have an equal tick count, then the hop count is used to determine the preferred path.

IPX Service Advertising Protocol (SAP) is a protocol for network resources, not a routing protocol, used to advertise addresses and services that are provided by devices, such as file and print servers.

It is the companion protocol to IPX RIP where SAP focuses on the services while RIP focuses on the networks. SAP advertisements are sent every 60 seconds and the routers will receive the advertisements, add them to the SAP table, and broadcast the table from their interfaces.

Link State

Link State Routing Protocols are more complex than distance vector and were created to overcome some limitations of distance vector routing protocols. With link state routing protocols, routers create their own information including IP addresses, connected links, and the state of each link. This information is sent from router to router. Each router will maintain a map of the network and calculate the best paths to a destination independently from the other routers.

Link state routing protocols send small updates about the state of links and are usually more CPU and memory intensive. Existing link state routing protocols include:

- IP Open Shortest Path First (OSPF)
- CLNS and IP Intermediate System-to-Intermediate System (IS-IS)
- DEC DNA Phase V
- IPX NetWare Link services Protocol (NLSP).

Open Shortest Path First (OSPF) is a link state routing protocol where each router sends advertisements on the link states to all other routers on the network. It is a classless routing protocol and allows

VLSM. Equal-cost load balancing is supported, as well as route authentication. The metric used for OSPF is cost. Cost is an unsigned 19-bit integer ranging from 1 to 65535. The default cost is calculated based on the bandwidth used by the interface.

OSPF introduces the concepts of areas, border routes, and designated routers. There are several link state advertisement (LSA) types defined by OSPF:

- Type Code 1 Router LSA
  Produced by every router and includes all the links, interfaces, link states, and cost of the router
- Type Code 2 Network LSA
  Produced by every designated router (DR) on every transit broadcast or nonbroadcast multiaccess (NBMA) network and lists all attached routers in the multiaccess network
- Type Code 3 Summary LSA for ABRs
  Produced by area border routers (ARBs) and sent into an area to advertise destinations outside the area
- Type Code 4 Summary LSA for ASBRs
  Starting with area border routers (ARBs) and advertises autonomous system boundary routers (ASBRs)
- Type Code 5 Autonomous System External LSA
  Starting with ASBRs and advertises destinations external to the OSPF autonomous system (AS) through flooding the OSPF AS
- Type Code 7 Not-so-stubby area External LSA
  Starting with ASBRs in not-so-stubby area (NSSA) and

advertises destinations external to the OSPF autonomous system to the NSSA directly without flooding the OSPF AS.

Areas are used by OSPF to reduce the effects of initial flooding and data maintenance of LSAs which can burden the router's CPU. Areas are logical grouping of routers and links dividing the network. Link-state information is shared between routers in their areas, reducing the size of the database. Area 0 is reserved for the backbone area and responsible for distributing routing information between areas.

Intra-area traffic is comprised of packets being passed between routers within a single area while inter-area traffic is packets passed between routers in different areas. Stub areas describe a configuration to an area which prevents OSPF external LSAs from being flooded into that area, namely type 5 LSAs. Totally Stubby Areas set the configuration so that a router has to go through a specific route to other areas or external networks, resulting in preventing type 3 or type 5 flooding. Not-So-Stubby Areas will retain the characteristics of a stub area while allowing external type 7 LSAs into the OSPF system.

Several router types are must be considered when using OSPF, including:

- Internal Router – routers whose interfaces belong to the same OSPF area and keep only one link-state database
- Area border router (ABR) – routers that are connected to more than one area and will maintain a link-state database

for each area they belong to

- Autonomous system boundary router (ASBR) – routers that inject external link-state advertisements into the OSPF database and the external routes are learned through static routed or other routing protocols
- Backbone router – routers with at least one interface to Area 0.

A single router can be an ABR, ASBR, or backbone router at the same time.

Designated Routers are found on multiaccess networks for the purpose of receiving the LSAs from all routers for broadcasting a type 2 network LSA. The decision for assigning a designated router, or backup designated router, is performed by the network.

NetWare Link-Services Protocol (NLSP) is a link-state routing protocol to overcome the limitations of RIP/SAP. It has characteristics similar to other link-state protocols. NLSP will support up to 127 hops and permits hierarchical routing with area, domain, and global internetworking components. In the context of NLSP, an area is a connection of connected networks with the same area address. A domain is a collection of areas. A global internetwork is a collection of domains. Hierarchical addressing is supported where each area is identified by a 32-bit address and a 32-bit mask similar to IP address masking.

Intermediate System to Intermediate System (IS-IS) is a link-state routing protocol used to determine the best way to forward datagrams through a packet-switched network. It is conceptually similar to OSPF, but does not use IP to carry routing information messages. IS-IS will classify routers as:

- Level 1 – Intra-area routers that form relationships with other Level 1 routers
- Level 2 – Inter-area routers that form relationships with other Level 2 routers
- Level 1-2 – will form relationships with routers on either level.

Hybrid

The Enhanced Interior Gateway Routing Protocol is a distance vector protocol that acts like a link state routing protocol and is considered a hybrid.

Enhanced Interior Gateway Routing Protocol (EIGRP) is considered a scalable routing protocol. It is a classless protocol permitting VLSMs, route authentication and supernetting. Routing updates are not performed periodically. EIGRP will autosummarize networks at borders and will load balance over unequal cost paths.

The metrics used for EIGRP are a more granular version of IGRP using bandwidth, delay, load, reliability, and MTU. Diffusing Update Algorithm (DUAL) is implemented to prevent routing loops.

EIGRP is a hybrid protocol with characteristics of both distance vector and link state. It will advertise its routing table to neighboring routers but will form neighbor relationships. EIGRP is only found on Cisco routers.

Updates are sent only when necessary and only to those routers requiring new information. Hello packets are used to learn about neighboring routers. On most networks, the interval between hello packets is 5 seconds. On multipoint networks with link speeds slower than T1, the hello packets are unicast every 60 seconds.

Designated Ports

A port is a software construction of specific applications or processes which are used as a communications endpoint of Transport Layer protocols. A specific port is identified by its number, the IP address it is associated with, and the protocol used.

A port number is a 16-bit unsigned integer ranging from 0 to 65535. A process will bind with a particular port to send and receive data. The port will listen for incoming packets that match the destination port number and the IP destination address or send outgoing packets with the source port number. Some processes may bind to multiple ports.

Processes will implement connections to ports using sockets: a software structure created by the process and bound to a socket address. The socket address is a combination of a port number and an IP address. Sockets are either half-duplex or full duplex; that is, they will send and receive data one direction at a time or in both directions simultaneously.

Port scanning is a technique of attempting to connect to a wide range of services on a single computer in sequence. This is possible because different services will commonly listen on different port numbers.

Port numbers are divided into three categories:

- Well Known Ports – 0 to 1023
- Registered Ports – 1024 to 49151
- Dynamic and Private Ports – 49152 to 65535

Common TCP Ports

- Port 8 – ICMP (Ping)
- Port 20 – FTP (data)
- Port 21 – FTP (control)
- Port 22 – SSH
- Port 23 – Telnet
- Port 25 – STMP
- Port 53 – DNS
- Port 69 – TFTP
- Port 80 – HTTP
- Port 110 – POP3
- Port 115 – SFTP
- Port 119 – NNTP
- Port 153 – SGMP

- Port 161 – SNMP
- Port 427 – SLP
- Port 443 – HTTPS

Common UDP Ports

- Port 8 – ICMP (Ping)
- Port 22 – SSH
- Port 25 – STMP
- Port 53 – DNS
- Port 67 – BOOTP/DHCP
- Port 69 – TFTP
- Port 80 – HTTP
- Port 123 – NTP
- Port 153 – SGMP
- Port 161 – SNMP
- Port 427 – SLP
- Port 443 – HTTPS

Operations Security

Address Formats

Several forms of addressing are used to distinguish devices on the network. The most commonly used formats are:

- IPv4
- IPv6
- MAC Address.

Internet Protocol (IP)

The Internet Protocol is a connection-less protocol used on packet-switched Link Layer networks. The protocol does not guarantee delivery, proper sequencing, nor avoid duplication, but relies on upper layer transport protocols, such as TCP to handle that. IP, however, does provide header integrity achieved with a checksum.

Addressing is one of the major contributions of the IP specification.

IPv4

IPv4 uses 32-bit addresses written normally in dot-decimal notation consisting of four octets separated by a period. Over a billion unique addresses are possible through this schema. An IP address is divided into a Network ID and host ID. All hosts on the same network have the same network ID. Classes of networks have been defined to allow a greater number of networks to be available. The specific classes are defined by:

- Class A – range of 1.0.0.0 to 126.0.0.0, where the first octet is the network number and the remaining octets are the host address
- Class B – range from 128.0.0.0 to 191.255.0.0, where the first two octets represent the network number and the remaining octets are the host number
- Class C – range from 192.0.1.0 to 223.255.255.0, where the first three octets are the network number and the last octet is the host number
- Class D – are reserved as multicast addresses and range

from 224.0.0.1 to 239.255.255.255

- Class E – are reserved for experimental networks and range from 240.0.0.0 to 254.0.0.0

Though the IP address is typically represented using dotted decimal notation, it can also be represented in binary and Classless Interdomain Routing (CIDR) notations.

Binary formatting utilizes a 2-based numeral system, or bits within groupings of 8. Reading right to left, each bit is twice the value of the preceding bit.

Examples

0000 0000 = 0

1111 1111 = 255

1111 0000 = 240

0000 1111 = 15

1010 1010 = 170

0101 0101 = 85

Binary translation

Code	1	1	1	1	1	1	1	1
Value	128	64	32	16	8	4	2	1

In dotted decimal format, xxx.xxx.xxx.xxx, the IP address can be represented in decimal (base 10) and hexadecimal (base 16) format. The addresses correlate to the binary address as such:

255.255.255.255 = 1111 1111.1111 1111.1111 1111.1111 1111

255.126.170.192 = 1111 1111.0111 1110.1010 1010.1100 0000

The strict rules of IP addressing cause a problem resulting in unused addresses. The description of the problem is shown through the following scenarios:

- A class C address range allows 254 hosts: a company of 40 hosts, 214 addresses would be wasted in the subnet
- A class B address range allows 65,534 hosts: a company of 4000 hosts, 61,534 addresses would be wasted in the subnet
- A class A address range allows 16,777,214 hosts: a company of 400,000 hosts, 16,377,214 addresses would be wasted in the subnet.

Class-less based IP addressing allows the default subnet mask to be extended which will change the representation of the host and network IDs. In a class B situation, extending the subnet mask by 2 bits, the host ID as 10 bits, while the network ID has 22 bits: the subnet is 255.255.192.0.

To calculate the number of host IDs supported by the new subnet, use the formula '2^n-2' where n is the number of bits used for the host ID, so in the example above (2^{10}-2). To calculate the number of network IDs supported by the new subnet, use the formula '2^n-2' where n is the number of bits used for the network ID, so in the example above (2^{22}-2).

Though IP addresses are reallocated, routing tables have a problem reading the new subnet mask. To resolve the problem, a new format is required; hence the Classless Interdomain Routing (CIDR) Notation. CIDR Notation uses the Dotted Decimal Format and the number of bits used for the network ID.

> 255.255.192.1 would be written 255.255.192.1/22 or
> 1111 1111.1111 1111.1111 1100.0000 0000

> 192.23.4.15/18 would be have a subnet notation is dotted decimal as
> 1111 1111.1111 1111.1100 0000.0000 0000

CIDR is used within the Internet; within an organization, Variable-length subnet mask (VLSM) is used. VLSM is used to manage the number of hosts available in a subnetwork. VLSM requires routing protocol supports sending of the subnet mask.

IPv6

IPv6 provides support to the unexpected growth of the Internet through a 128-bit address divided along 16-bit boundaries. Each 16-bit segment converts to a 4-digit hexadecimal number with a colon separating each number. The form of the address is

> xxxx:xxxx:xxxx:xxxx:xxxx:xxxx:xxxx:xxxx.

Zero-suppression makes address reading easier by removing any leading zeros from the address.

A subnet mask is not required with IPv6 because it uses a fixed prefix that contains specific routing and subnet information.

The benefits of IPv6 over IPv4 are:

- Large address space – provides every device on the Internet with a globally unique address
- Efficient routing – supports hierarchical routing infrastructures
- Straightforward configuration – uses Dynamic Host Configuration Protocol for IPv6 (DHCPv6) and local routers for automatic IP configuration
- Enhanced security – provides better protection against address and port scanning attacks.

The subnet size for IPv6 is standardized to have a fixed host ID portion of 64 bites which will facilitate automatic formation of the host ID from the Link Layer MAC address.

IPv6 addresses are classified into three types:

- Unicast addresses – identifies a single network interface
- Anycast addresses – assigned to a group of interfaces belonging to different nodes on the network. Delivery of a packet goes to the closest member interface
- Multicast addresses – assigned to a group of interfaces belonging to different nodes on the network. Delivery of a packet goes to all the interfaces identified in the address.

To support translations and allow for networks to have both IPv4 and IPv6 addressing, the addressing format can be merged. Since the IPv4 address uses 32 bits, it uses the last two 16 bit segments of the IPv6 address. The formatted address would look like:

xxxx:xxxx:xxxx:xxxx:xxxx:xxxx:yyy.yyy.yyy.yyy

Some IPv6 stacks will not support this mapped address feature.

MAC Address

The Media Access Control (MAC) address is a unique identifier assigned to network adapters and network interface cards by the manufacturer. The Institute of Electrical and Electronics Engineers (IEEE) manage three numbering spaces that are commonly used to formulate a MAC address: MAC-48, EUI-48, and EUI-64. Though intended to be permanent and a globally unique method of identification, the MAC address can be changed.

The most common form of representing a MAC address is six groups (octets or bytes) of two hexadecimal digits separated by hyphens or colons. The form of the notation appears as:

xx:xx:xx:xx:xx:xx

Each byte of the address represents 8 bits. The first three octets represent an Organizationally Unique Identifier (OUI) while the remaining three octets represent the specific Network Interface Card (NIC). These are considered universally administered address.

A network administrator can override the burned-in address and assign a locally administered address which does not contain OUIs.

Addressing Technologies

Subnetting

Subnetting is a method used to determine the network, subnetwork, and hosts of an IP address. The default mask can be manipulated to create subnetworks for the LAN and WAN segments. Each call has a default address mask, which is a 32-bit string. The Network-layer devices use the IP address and the mask to determine which network portion the address belongs.

By converting the IP address and Mask into their binary notation and performing an XOR function, the subnetwork can be discovered.

There are two methods for representing the subnet mask. The first is the dotted decimal, such as 255.255.255.0. The second is the bit mask number format which displays the number of bits in the subnet: 255.255.255.0 is represented as /24 because it has 24 bits.

In some cases, the number of available IP addresses on a network exceeds the number of computers. This is especially true for point-to-point serial connections. The additional unused IP addresses would be wasted. Variable length subnet masks (VLSM) allow different masks to be used for different segments in the network.

Using subnet masking, a large Class B network can be divided into smaller subnetworks. A /23 mask will create eight subnetworks; each network handling 510 hosts. One of these subnetworks can be divided even further with a /30 mask to provide 128 subnetworks to allow for serial links.

Supernetting

Where subnetting is used to divide IP addresses groups into smaller, more manageable groups, supernetting is a method for grouping networks into larger supernets through borrowing bits from the network portion of the address. This is especially important when the number of computers on a network exceed the number of addresses available, for example Class C networks with available 254 addresses.

By grouping two Class C networks together using supernets, more IP addresses are available. When two classful networks are grouped into a supernet, routing is now considered classless.

Address aggregation is a method of summarizing routing entries of a set of classful networks.

Classless Interdomain Routing (CIDR) is a function of Internet Border Gateway Protocol (BGP) routing to reduce the number of Class C routes from an autonomous system. This prevents several broadcast messages each going to a single Class C network from being sent out to the next router. Instead, a single broadcast message is sent to the autonomous system where it sends the message to the different networks.

Public and Private Addresses

Some addresses within the classes have been reserved for private use by companies in their internal network. These addresses cannot be routed to the Internet and are filtered out by Internet service providers. The private addresses in each of the classes are:

- Class A – 10.0.0.0 to 10.255.255.255
- Class B – 172.16.0.0 to 172.31.255.255
- Class C – 192.168.0.0 to 192.168.255.255

To connect to the Internet, a computer needs a globally unique IP address which is registered. For organizations, the IP address is used for Internet access and access to the organization's network. RFC 1918 provides a set of unregistered network numbers that are not used in the public domain, but can be used by organization for internal use.

Network Access Translation

RFC 1631 defines Network Access Translation, which allows organizations to use a private IP address on an internal network and the Internet at the same time. This is done by using a valid registered IP address to represent the private address on the Internet.

Several variations of NAT are supported:

- Static NAT
- Dynamic NAT
- Overloading NAT with Port Address Translation (PAT).

With Static NAT, the IP addresses are statically mapped to each other, creating a one-to-one relationship between the registered address and the private address.

With Dynamic NAT, the one-to-one relationship between the registered address and the private address still exists. The registered addresses, or global addresses, are part of a pool of IP addresses which are dynamically used. Dynamic NAT defines criteria for determining how private addresses, or local addresses, should be translated.

With Dynamic NAT, an organization can have more local addresses than global addresses. When a packet arrives that needs a NAT entry, a global address is retrieved from the pool and associated to the local address. If no global address is available, the packet is discarded.

Port Address Translation (PAT)

Overloading allows NAT to support clients with a few global addresses. Port Address Translation (PAT) will translate the port number in addition to the IP address. With dynamic mapping, NAT provides a global IP address, but also a unique port number associated with that address. The NAT router keeps a table entry for every unique combination of local addresses and ports. With a 16-bit field for port numbers, overloading NAT provides more than 65,000 port numbers.

Though an organization has access to private addresses registered to them, they can also utilize network numbers registered to another organization. NAT will translate the source and destination IP addresses of two organizations using a network number if they are connected to the Internet. As the packet passes through the NAT router, the source and destination addresses are changed.

Dynamic Host Configuration Protocol (DHCP)

Using Dynamic Host Configuration Protocol, a configured client will send a broadcast query when connecting to the network. The query requests information from a DHCP server which is managing a pool of IP addresses and information about appropriate client configuration parameters. When a valid request is received from the DHCP server, the client is assigned an IP address, a lease for the address, and other IP configuration parameters that the client must adhere to.

DHCP operations involve four distinct phases:

- IP Discovery
- IP Lease Offer
- IP Request
- IP Lease Acknowledgment.

Within the DHCP discovery phase, the client broadcasts a message on the physical subnet to identify any available DHCP servers. The message is a UDP packet and is commonly referred to as the DHCPDISCOVER message. If one is not available, network administrators will have to configure any local routers to forward

DHCP packets to a DHCP server on another subnet.

DHCP clients can request their last-known IP address. If the client remains connected to the network where this IP address is valid, the server has the option to assign the request. If the server is authoritative, it can deny the request and force the client to request a new IP address, or ignore the request leading to a timeout for the client and forcing a new IP address to be requested.

In the DHCP offer phase, the server receives the request from the client and reserves an IP address for the client and an IP lease offer. This is performed through a DHCPOFFER message back to the client. Within the message, the server will note the client's MAC address, the IP address that is being offered, the subnet mask, the duration of the lease, and the IP address of the DHCP server making the offer.

The client will receive DHCP offers from multiple services and accept only one. Once an offer is accepted the, client will broadcast a DHCP request message (DHCPREQUEST) to all DHCP servers. The broadcasted message informs the DHCP servers on which offer the client accepted, which allow each server to withdraw the offers that were not accepted and returned the reserved IP address to the pool.

After receiving the DHCPREQUEST message from the client, the DHCP server will reply with a DHCPACK packet to the client, acknowledging the process is complete.

Network Scanning

Network scanning typically involves making request to systems and networking elements to determine what services are being offered or are filtering. It is used to detect 'live' systems on a target network to:

- Determine the perimeter of the target network or system
- Facilitate network mapping
- Build an inventory of accessible systems.

Scanning is used to determine the availability of a system on the network. Scanning tools gather information about a system such as IP addresses, operating systems and services which may be running on the system. 'Live' is a term referring to networked devices that are available, responsive, and open to attack.

Since scanning can provide enormous amounts of information about a network, it is often a tool used by hackers and malicious attackers. Therefore, countermeasures are usually implemented. Countermeasures are the processes and tools sets used to detect and prevent malicious activity.

Port scanning refers to gathering information about open TCP/IP ports and services on the system. Port numbers are associated with services or applications on a machine. Port scanning tools allow the services available on a given system to be identified.

The most commonly known ports are:

20 FTP data

21	FTP controlled
22	Secure Shell (SSH)
23	Telnet
25	SMTP
39	RLP
53	DNS
80	HTTP
88	Kerberos
110	POP3
115	SFTP
118	SQL
137	NetBIOS Name Service
138	NetBIOS Datagram Service
139	NetBIOS Session Service
143	IMAP
156	SQL Service
161	SNMP
194	IRC
443	HTTP over TLS/SSL
444	SNPP
445	SMB over TCP/IP
593	HTTP RPC

Network scanning focuses on identifying IP addresses looking for active hosts on the network for purposes of security assessments. Network hosts are identified by their IP addresses. Network scanning tools look for all live or hosts on the network and their IP addresses.

Vulnerability scanning attempts to identify weaknesses within the current system. Typically, this will identify the operating system and version number, including any installed service packs. With this information, the vulnerability scanning looks for any weaknesses in the operating system which can be exploited later.

Active port-scanning activity can be detected using an intrusion detection system (IDS). Scans can be recognized when they probe TCP/IP ports.

A passive scan is used to identify open application ports on remote systems and happens during communication setup. A SYN packet is sent to the target system on a specific application port. The desired result is a response:

- An acknowledgment indicates the port is open and the service is accepting connections
- A reset identifies the port as closed or being filtered
- No response typically means the port is being blocked, especially when other ports are responding. The reply is dropped with no acknowledgment of receipt.

Active scans are similar to passive scans, but are used to discover ghost open ports, such as a firewall or load-balancing system. The reply is not dropped and an acknowledgment of the reply is sent. The purpose is to test the ability to establish communications with the remote system.

Interactive scans will connect to the service and exchange commands and response. Its primary purpose is to learn about the system

Command Line Interface Tool

Several tools are available to network administrators from the command line interface to identify and diagnose problems which occur. Some sophisticated graphic-enhance tools may utilize these same command line tools to perform some of the same functions.

The most useful command line interface tools are:

- traceroute – used to determine the route taken by packets across an IP network to a specified destination
- ipconfig – used to display all current TCP/IP network configuration information as well as refresh the DHCP and DNS settings of a computer. (for Windows)
- ifconfig – used to configure, control, and query TCP/IP network interface parameters. (for UNIX-like operating systems)
- ping – used to identify if a network device is available on the network and to perform a self-test on the NIC of the computer
- Arp – similar to the ping tool but operates at the OSI Link Layer using the Address Resolution Protocol (ARP)
- Nslookup – used to query DNS servers to find detailed information about IP addresses, MX records, and NS servers
- MTR – combines the functions of traceroute and ping

programs into a single network diagnostic tool. It probes routers on the route path and listens for their responses to identify response times for the individual hops

- NBTstat – a diagnostic tool for NetBIOS over TCP/IP
- Netstat – displays network connections, routing tables, and other network interface statistics.

IDS Overview

Intrusion detection systems (IDS) utilize various techniques to alert organizations to adverse or unwanted activity. IDS can be implemented as a network device (NIDS) or into a host system (HIDS)

Intrusion prevention systems (IPS) block all unwanted processes, allowing only allowed functions and actions on the network or system. IPS can be also implemented on the network (NIPS) or host (HIPS)

Intrusion Detection Systems

An IDS is a reactive warning system meant to provide information to administration to make decisions to respond to an attack. Developments in technology have allowed some responses to predefined attacks to be automated under limited conditions.

The unique traffic generated by the organization will require the IDS to be tuned to support the network. If tuned incorrectly, the IDS can create a significant vulnerability for the organization.

A Network Intrusion Detection System (NIDS) will monitor the traffic traveling on the network segment which the system is attached. A passive NIDS is attached to a hub using a network tap or mirroring the ports on a switch to a NIDS dedicated port. The system will inspect all packets and monitor sessions without impact.

NIDS have several essential characteristics:

- Monitors network packets and traffic in real time
- Analyzes protocols and other packet information
- Can send alerts or terminate offending connections
- Can integrate with firewalls and define rules
- Monitoring data packets can be disrupted by encryption.

Host-based intrusion detection systems (HIDS) are implemented at the host level. The intrusion detection analysis is the primary difference from NIDS. The scope of the HIDS is the boundaries of the host, and increases the level of visibility and control available because of its integration with the host.

Some HIDS have the ability to monitor multiple hosts and will share policy information and real-time information between systems.

The characteristics of HIDS include:

- Apparent intrusions can be detected on the host
- Event logs, critical system files, and other auditable systems resources can be scrutinized
- Monitors for unauthorized changes or suspicious behavior patterns

- Alerts are sent when unusual events are detected
- Multihost HIDS will receive audit data from multiple hosts.

Analysis Engine Methods

An IDS can utilize several analysis methods. Two basic types include:

- Pattern matching - the attack vector is known and an alert is provided when the pattern is detected
- Anomaly detection – draws conclusions from the use of several tactics to determine if the traffic represents a risk.

Pattern matching technology was utilized by some of the first IDS products and was based on signatures – collections of byte sequences that represented a mode of attack. A single database in a pattern matching IDS would have hundreds, or thousands, of signatures.

Some attributes of a pattern matching IDS include:

- Known attacks are identified
- Specific information for analysis and response is provided
- False-positives may be triggered
- Signatures need to be updated regularly
- Attacks may be modified to avoid detection.

Another form of pattern matching is stateful matching where the IDS scan for attack signatures within the traffic stream rather than the individual packets. The main difference from basic pattern matching is that signatures are detected across multiple packets.

Anomalies can include:

- Users logging in at strange hours
- Unusual error messages
- Unexplained system shutdowns or restarts
- Unexplained changes to system checks
- Multiple failed log-on attempts.

Statistical anomaly-based IDS will analyze the audit trail data by comparing to predicted profiles to find potential breaches. The main advantage of anomaly-based solutions is that they can detect unknown attacks.

The attributes for statistical anomaly- based IDS are:

- A baseline for normal traffic and throughputs is developed and monitored against
- DoS floods and unknown attacks can be detected
- Tuning the system properly can be difficult
- The normal traffic conditions must be clearly understood.

A protocol anomaly-based IDS will use known protocols to determine any unacceptable behavior. The benefits of this form of IDS are directly impacted by the use of well-defined protocols.

Protocol anomaly-based IDS have attributes such as:

- Deviations from standards set by request for comments (RFC) are monitored

- Attacks no having signatures can be identified
- Well-defined protocols can reduce the number of false-positives
- Protocol analysis has a longer deployment time than signatures.

Analysis of the traffic structure can identify unaccepted deviation from expected behaviors and is employed by traffic anomaly-based IDS. The specific attributes include:

- Watches for new services or unusual traffic patterns
- DoS floods and unknown attacks can be identified
- Tuning the system can be difficulty
- The normal traffic conditions must be clearly understood.

Intrusion Responses

The responses from an IDS include:

- Dropping suspicious data packets at the firewall
- Denying access because of suspicious activity
- Reporting activity to other hosts
- Updating the configurations within the IDS.

Alarms are the primary capability of an IDS. There are three fundamental components to alarms:

- Sensor
- Control and communication
- Alert/enunciator/actuator.

The sensor detects the event and produces the necessary notification.

The mechanism of distribution is the control and communication of the alarm which determines if the alert is sent through e-mail, pager, instant message, or the like.

The enunciator acts as a relay station ensuring that the proper people are alerted at the appropriate time. This assumes that not all people need to be alerted at the same time.

Security Management Practices

Security Threats

Any threat against the confidentiality, integrity, and availability of enterprise assets is a threat to access control.

Recognized threats to access control consist of:

- Denial of service
- Buffer overflows
- Mobile code
- Malicious software
- Password cracker
- Spoofing/masquerading
- Sniffers
- Eavesdropping
- Emanations
- Shoulder surfing
- Tapping
- Object reuse
- Data remnants
- Unauthorized targeted data mining
- Dumpster diving
- Backdoor/trapdoor
- Theft
- Intruders
- Social engineering.

Denial of Service (DoS)

Denial of service attacks consist of:

- Consuming specific resources
- System services or applications becoming unusable by users
- Total failure of a system.

In the early 1990s, the most prevalent attacks were SYN attacks; TCP/IP protocol manipulation caused when an overwhelming number of open-ended session requests would be sent to a service, causing the service to focus on processing these requests while delaying legitimate requests. The result was that systems were virtually unusable by valid users and applications of the service.

Denial of service is typically a result of finding a weakness in system services and exploiting that weakness. One of the most common characteristic of a DoS attack is the use of multiple events, systems, or users to focus legitimate actions against a single system. The result is a manipulation of system interactions for the purpose of acquiring access of redirect communications.

Buffer Overflows

A portion of memory is usually allocated to temporarily store information that is used for processing. This is called a buffer and is essential to manage data input and outputs during system interaction.

A buffer overflow is a manipulation of the system's ability to manage the buffer which, in turn, causes a system failure such as an outage, failure to control the application state, or failure to control the data required for processing.

Poor system memory access control and management is the typical cause of buffer overflows. Proper coding of the application, services, and operating systems managing the memory allocation is a good start at preventing this threat. Adequate testing in the development process can ensure that the coding is done properly and identify any vulnerability to buffer overflows.

Mobile Code

Any software that is transmitted across a network from a remote source to a local system and executed without any explicit action from the user is referred to as mobile code. The local system can be a personal computer, smart device, PDA, mobile phone, or Internet appliance. Mobile code does not need to be installed or executed by the user and is typically known as downloadable code and active content.

Mobile code is not necessarily harmful and includes:

- ActiveX controls
- Java applets
- Browser scripts
- HTML e-mail.

However, significant security implications surround mobile code because of the capabilities of dynamic distribution, limited user awareness, and potential for harm. Mobile code used maliciously can track user activity, access vital information or install other applications without the user's knowledge. To prevent malicious mobile code, the system has to be configured properly.

Malicious Software

Malicious software is used to describe Trojans or spyware, but has expanded to include any software, application, applet, script, or digital material run on a computer system that can be a threat to the system, applications, or information.

Falling into the category of malicious software, or malware, is:

- Viruses – parasitic code which requires human assistance to transfer or insert into the system or is attached to another program to allow replication and distribution.
- Worms – self-propagating code which exploit vulnerabilities in systems or applications. Similar to viruses without the need for human interaction.
- Trojan Horses – any program that appears to the user as desirable but is, in the end, harmful.
- Spyware – hidden applications intended to track user's activity, obtain personal data, and even monitor system inputs.

Password Crackers

Passwords are a grouping of secret characters used to prove the identity of the user. Passwords are prone to discovering and given that they range from an average or 5 to 15 characters, they are limited by the number of potential combinations of characters.

Passwords are stored by a one-way hash, an algorithm producing a unique representation of the password. When a system receives a hashed password, it uses the same algorithm used to create the password and compares it the hash on file. If the hash is correct, the certainty that the password provided is on file increases. In most cases, the password is never stored or saved, only the hash.

Password crackers work on the hashed password which has been saved. When the file containing the hashed password is found, the password cracker compared every possible password combination against the hash. This is done by using or creating a list of possible combinations, hash them, and compare the hash to stored password on the file. The length and complexity of the password has an impact on the time required to test every combination, ranging from minutes to years.

Password crackers are easily obtainable and are useful for both hackers and system administrators. System administrators use password crackers to identify the strength of a particular password. If the password is weak, a request can be made to the user to change to a stronger password.

In 1980, Martin Hellman described a method of using pre-calculated data stored in memory to reduce the time required for cryptanalysis. By performing an exhaustive search and loading results into memory, time required to create a list for use by password crackers can be significantly decreased. This is commonly referred to as a time-memory tradeoff, where saving memory and the cost of processing time compete with each other.

Many password hashes are generated by encrypting a fixed plaintext with the user's password as the key. A poorly designed password hashing scheme will result in the plaintext and encryption method being the same for all passwords. This allows password hashes to be calculated in advance and subjecting them to a time-memory tradeoff.

The Hellman concept is based on enciphering the plaintext with all possible keys whose results are organized into chains. Only the first and last elements are loaded into memory. As the number of stored chains increased, so did the frequency of generating the same results with different keys.

By 1982, Ron Rivest had introduced the concept of distinguishing points which improved simple password hashes by reducing the number of memory lookups. The distinguishing points were defined at the ends of the chains based on the fact that the first ten bits of the key were all zeros. When a plausible match is identified, a chain is pulled from memory from the end. Focus on the distinguishing points at the end reduced the time required to process passwords.

A faster time-memory trade-off was developed by Philippe Oechslin in 2003. The issue with the chaining process was the possibility of collision between chains and eventual mergers within memory. To limit the collision rates and reduce memory requirements, Oechslin proposed an approach to the creation of chains. His new chain structure was called rainbow chains and utilized the distinguished points concept with a process for successive reduction of points.

Spoofing/Masquerading

An attack method utilizing weaknesses with Internet protocols to gain access to systems based on IP addresses and inherent trust relationships were first conceived by Steve Bellovin. But Kevin Mitnick popularized the concept of IP spoofing in the 1980s. IP spoofing allows a person to appear to come from a trusted source when they are actually outside of the trusted environment.

Earlier versions of spoofing were performed at the protocol layer by sending packets to the server with the source address of a known system in the packet header. Filtering devices would pass the packet if they were configured to permit activity to and from the trusted address or network. Though this would allow the packet to arrive, it did not guarantee the desired response from the server.

Modern systems and firewalls compensate for spoofing attacks. Similar attacks manipulating the trust of systems and users are still prevalent. Phishing is another form of masquerading as a trusted source. Domain Name Servers can be used to redirect Internet users from valid websites to malicious sites. Spoofing is used in man-in-the-middle attacks where users may believe they are interacting with a desired destination when in fact they have been redirected through an intermediary who is collecting information from both sides of the communication.

Spoofing or masquerading has significant impact on the access control environment since attackers gain access in such a way that circumvents the established controls.

Sniffers, Eavesdropping, and Tapping

At some point in networking between to computers, communications will pass through a physical device. Gaining access to the physical device could provide insight into all layers of communication, in the form of eavesdropping or tapping.

The same capabilities are utilized by IDSs which monitor communications in an effort to detect unwanted activities.

Sniffers are devices collecting information from a communication medium.

Emanations

Emanation is a proliferation or propagation of a signal which is most evident in wireless networks. By being within range of the wireless signal, an attacker can attempt to access the network without physically accessing the facility.

Emanations can be tapped to allow eavesdropping. The key is tapping into the electromagnetic properties of computing devices to acquire data from a distance.

Encryption of signals can provide some protection. Reducing the emanation of a signal can also provide some protection using mechanisms such as TEMPEST.

Shoulder Surfing

Shoulder surfing is a form of social engineering where information is gathered through direct observation. Watching a person entering a password or listening to a conversation containing sensitive information are forms of shoulder surfing.

Deterrents to shoulder surfing include:

- Awareness training
- One-time use passwords
- Multifactor authentication
- Screen filters
- Special polarized glasses.

Object Reuse

The allocation or reallocation of system resources to an application or process is referred to as object reuse. In essence, applications and services create objects which are stored in memory. Those objects can be used over and over by the application or services that are shared with other applications and services. An object used to perform a privileged task for an application or authorized user. If the usage of this object is not controlled and remains in memory, it can become available to unauthorized use.

Application object reuse has two aspects:

- The direct employment of the object
- The use of input or output data from the object.

To protect against the harmful reuse of an entire object, an application should erase all residual data from the object before it is assigned to another process to prevent the data from being intentionally or unintentionally read.

Security requires a controlled sharing of object resources. Since these resources are in memory, their management can be difficult. Many systems are running multiple processes simultaneously. Memory may be allocated to one process for a while, deallocated and reallocated to another process making the constant processing a potential security vulnerability. This is because residual information may still exist in a memory section when it is reallocated to a new process.

The same concern is applicable to system media like hard drives, magnetic media, and other forms of data storage. It is common practice to reuse media to reduce costs in backup activities. Removing all data from the media ensures that proprietary and confidential information is not compromised. Standard methods include:

- Degaussing
- Writing over media.

Data Remanence

Similar to object reuse is data remanence, which is often seen when used computer equipment is reused or sold to another user. The partial or entire remains of digital information still exist for the new user.

Hard drives are comprised of platters organized into segments and clusters. When files are written to the hard drive, it is placed in one or more clusters in a series of spread across the disk. The file allocation table is responsible for tracking the physical location information for the file in order to retrieve it later.

Several situations can lead to data exposure:

- Deleting a file removes the information from the file allocation table but not from the physical cluster
- Sensitive or confidential data is stored in the slack space of partially used clusters and remains until the entire cluster is overwritten with new data
- Malicious information or code is stored by attackers within the slack space.

The most effective mechanism to destroy data is to overwrite the data several times:

- Providing enough randomization to prevent statistical analysis of the data
- Further masking the remnants of any electromagnetic representation of the data with each rewrite.

Unauthorized Targeted Data Mining

Any collection of large amounts of information for the purpose of creating predictions is considered data mining. There are several reasons for data mining information and is often used to provide a logical determination about the information over specific data.

Hackers generally perform reconnaissance in order to collect as much information as possible to determine the operations, practices, technical architecture, and business cycles. Though individual pieces of data may be harmless, different combinations of data could be created and analyzed to identify vulnerabilities that can be exploited.

One common area of concern is marketing; where security is concerned that public information that is placed on web sites cannot be used against the company. In the early days of the Internet, a large amount of data was posted by companies to the Internet that aided hackers in determining how and what to attack. Current awareness ensures that sensitive is not posted as easily, however the evolution of search engines have made sensitive information easier to discover.

Dumpster Diving

Dumpster diving is a simple tactic of rooting through trash to obtain enough information to create a strategy for attacking a target. The process is similar to data mining in stringing small data or insignificant data together to obtain a large, more harmful fact about the target.

Destroying documentation is one of the best chances against this vulnerability, as well as destruction of media to prevent exposure.

Backdoors and Trapdoors

Many creators of applications create special access capabilities into their software code for troubleshooting purposes. These created capabilities are commonly referred to as backdoors. If a person knows the location of the backdoor, then they can obtain access to the application or system without the knowledge of the system owner.

System Integrators create special rules and credentials to ensure they have complete access to the systems installed for the purpose of supporting their customer. Typically, the same methods and credentials are used for multiple customers. If a person was to obtain this information, they would have complete access over several customers' systems.

Theft

Physical theft is any item of value that an authorized person can remove. Digital theft does not require removal, but simply needs to be copied by an unauthorized person.

Social Engineering

Social Engineering is the use of coercion or misdirection to obtain information. It always consists of a degree of interaction, though that interaction may be on the telephone, through e-mail, or face-to-face.

E-mail social engineering is a common effort to use e-mail to obtain information. In most cases, an e-mail is sent disguised as coming from a trusted source. The message is a request for information. The victim believes they are sending the information to a source that has the right to know the information.

Help Desk fraud occurs when an attacker, poised as an employee, calls the Help Desk for assistance. The goal of the attack is usually to reset a password. In some cases, remote-access phone numbers or IP addresses can be obtained. Attackers will sometimes poise as managers to obtain special privileges.

Risk Management Overview

Risk is the possibility of loss.

Risk assessments evaluate:

- Potential threats
- Current vulnerabilities
- Probability and frequency

- Impact from risk exposure
- Identifying countermeasures
- Residual risks after implementing countermeasures.

Risk assessments fall into two categories:

- Qualitative
- Quantitative.

Qualitative Risk Assessments

Results of a qualitative risk assessment are descriptive over measurable. They are usually performed when:

- The expertise of quantitative risk assessments is limited
- The timeframe required to complete the assessment is short
- Data required to conduct a quantitative assessment is limited.

Qualitative risk assessments are typically performed by:

1. Gaining management approval.
2. Formulating an assessment team.
3. Gathering documentation on:
    - Strategy
    - Policies, procedures, guidelines, and baselines
    - Past assessments and audits
    - Technical documentation
    - Application development and operations documentation

- Business continuity and disaster recovery plans
- Security incident response documentation
- Data classification schemes
- Executive mandates.

4. Interviews conducted with managers and employees.

Quantitative Risk Assessments

Quantitative risk assessments focus on the interpretation of measurable data, covering:

- Frequency
- Probability
- Impact
- Countermeasure effectiveness.

Quantitative risk assessments are conducted through a simple process of:

1. Obtaining management approval.
2. Building an assessment team.
3. Review of information currently available within the organization.

Common Security Measurements

Simple calculations used in quantitative risk assessments include:

- Single loss expectancy (SLE)
- Annualized rate of occurrence (ARO)
- Annualized loss expectancy (ALE)

- Local annual frequency estimate (LAFE)
- Standard annual frequency estimate (SAFE).

Formulas used include:

SLE = asset value ($) * exposure factor (%)

ALE = ARO * SLE

Assessment Methodologies

Qualitative Assessments

- NIST SP 800-30
- NIST SP 800-66
- OCTAVE
- FRAP – Facilitated Risk Analysis Process
- CRAMM – CCTA Risk Analysis and Management Method.

Quantitative Assessments

- Spanning-Tree Analysis
- Failure Modes and Effect Analysis.

Principles of Risk Management

Risk Avoidance involves creating solutions that ensure a specific risk is not realized.

Risk Transfer will pass a specific risk to another entity.

Risk Mitigation attempts to eliminate or significantly decrease the level of risk present.

Risk Acceptance weighs the cost and benefits of handling the risks over accepting them.

Vulnerabilities and Threats

Threats in the Environment

Some threats in the application begin during development of the software and are exploited later. The most common threats in this form are:

- Buffer overflow – a program's memory buffer fills with more data than the buffer can hold, allowing the execution path to change or data to be written to other areas of memory including the operation system
- Citizen programmers – individuals without formal software development training programming
- Covert channel – two cooperating processes allowed to transfer information such that the security policy is violated. The two common types of covert channels are storage and timing
- Memory reuse/object reuse – unintended leaving or reuse of data or resources under conditions not beneficial to the proper operation of the application, such as paging or swap files
- Trapdoor/backdoor – programming mechanisms to allow full access to application code and resources when the

application crashes. These mechanisms can be exploited with serious consequences if found.

Malicious Attacks

Anti-virus and intrusion detection systems can detect and resolve most vulnerabilities and threats as long as they are regularly updated. The most common vulnerabilities and threats include:

- Viruses – malicious code that spreads from system to system based on intervention from the user
- Worms – similar to viruses without the requirement of user intervention
- Trojan horses – malicious code is hidden within legitimate programs with the intention of having the user execute it and run in the background
- Logic bombs – ties to a particular date, time, holiday, or system to wait until the event occurs to deliver the payload
- Denial of service – attempts to prevent legitimate use of systems by some form of disability, usually in the form of flooding the target system with excessive activity or specific exploits.

Protective Measures

Methods are available to attract malicious activity without harming the legitimate operations of the organization. The most commonly used are antivirus software and IDS/IPS solutions. More advanced solutions include:

- Honeypots are specifically designed to attract potential attackers for the purpose of studying their behaviors and activities and deflecting their attack on high value targets. Honeynets are networks of honeypots
- Darknets are monitored IP subnets. The advantage to these subnets are that no legitimate activity should exist allowing any activity to a destination address in the subnet can be considered malicious.

Operations Security

The goal of operations security is the protection and control of information assets. This is done through the implementation of security controls that provide transparent protection from harm or misuse.

Personnel

The roles and responsibilities for operational security falls into a number of groups, such as:

- Operators
- Users
- System administrators
- Security administrators
- System accounts.

Multiple Roles

Separating the control of security mechanisms is an effective method of preventing collusion.

Whenever possible, duties should be rotated to allow persons to work different assignments on a temporary basis. This enables greater understanding of the business operations and aids in identifying vulnerabilities.

Another method of deterring collusion is to require individuals to take at least one week of vacation each year. Extended absences from the office are opportunities to allow problems to arise that would normally not be seen when an individual is on duty.

Controls

All systems are a combination of several resources requiring some form of controls. Those systems are:

- Facilities
- Hardware
- Software
- Documentation.

Control Categories

Controls are normally divided into categories:

- Preventive controls stop an attack from succeeding

- Detective controls identify malicious activity
- Corrective controls restore a resource to the operational state before the disruption
- Directive control provide compliance to security strategies, legislation, and regulations
- Recovery controls support the business continuity strategies and systems
- Deterrent controls attempt to thwart an attack before it is made
- Compensating controls work with existing controls to supplement or augment.

Based on the Orange Book, controls are separated into two types of assurance mechanisms: operations and lifecycle.

Operational Assurance

Operational Assurance ensures the features and system architecture of the solution does not enable the security policy to be circumvented during system operations.

Some key focus areas to maintain operational assurance are:

- System architecture
- System integrity
- Covert channel analysis
- Trusted facility management
- Trusted recovery.

Four types of recovery are described by the Common Criteria:

- Manual recovery
- Automated recovery
- Automated recovery with undue loss
- Function recovery.

Lifecycle Assurance

Lifecycle Assurance ensures the proper steps are taken during the design, develop, and maintain the organization's controls and standards that are highly formal and rigorous.

Some of the processes considered are:

- Security testing
- Design specification and verification
- Configuration management
- Change control
- Problem management
- Software access control
- Patch management
- Library maintenance.

Change Control

Change management covers the entire lifecycle of a system and software. Every action that is perpetrated on a system must have gone through change control. The process entails:

1. Introducing a change

2. Cataloging the change
3. Scheduling the change
4. Implementing the change
5. Reporting the change to appropriate parties.

Auditing

Security audits serve to ensure compliance with the security policy. Different audits have different perspectives they handle, from organizational policies and accounting standards to legal and regulatory standards.

Audits can be conducted by internal or external groups; though to prevent undue influence in the audit, all audits should be performed by qualified personnel not associated with the security or operational functions.

Critical or sensitive systems should have audit trails that record events that place the system at harm, with the minimum information:

- Date and time of the event
- Person causing the event
- Details of the event-related activity
- Source of the event.

Operations Security (OPSEC)

OPSEC is a process of analysis where the organization's information is perceived from a competing organization's standpoint. The analysis determines:

- The organization's actions and information are visible to the competition
- Information obtained by the competition can be used and how
- Identifying selected measures for eliminating or reducing competitive exploitation of critical information.

The origins of OPSEC are based in military research to determine how enemies obtain sensitive information about military plans and what is required to prevent or mitigate such exploitation.

The steps of the process include:

- Identification of Critical Information – specifically finding information needed by the competition to allow the remainder of the process to focus on protecting this smaller subset of critical information
- Analysis of Threats – utilizes intelligence, counterintelligence, and open source information to determine key competitors and associates specific to a planned operation
- Analysis of Vulnerabilities – examines all aspects of a planned operation to identify appropriate OPSEC indicators and comparing them against the competitor's capabilities
- Assessment of Risk – matching vulnerabilities against preventative measures

- Application of Appropriate OPSEC Measures – implements the measures identified to resolve or mitigate vulnerabilities.

Security Architecture and Models

Core Security Principles

The principles of security which all security architecture is built around are:

- Confidentiality
- Integrity
- Availability.

Security Governance

IT governance defined by ITGI:
"A structure of relationships and processes to direct and control the enterprise in order to achieve the enterprise's goals by adding value while balancing risk versus return over IT and its processes."

IT governance intends to guarantee that appropriate security activities are performed to:

- Reduce risks appropriately
- Direct security investments
- Executive oversight
- Determining effectiveness of the program.

Confidentiality

Focused on ensuring proper access to information is authorized for:

- People

- Processes
- Systems.

Components of security that apply:

- Identification
- Authentication
- Authorization
- Encryption.

Integrity

Focuses on protecting information from changes which are:

- Intentional
- Unauthorized
- Accidental.

Controls in place to ensure accepted practices are used to modify information, including:

- Segregation of duties
- Approval checkpoints through life cycle
- Implementation of testing practices
- Limiting update access.

Availability

Focuses on the accessibility of information by users when needed.

Systems availability affected by:

- Lack of adequate security controls
- Loss of services due to disaster.

The impact of system downtime is based on:

- The criticality of the system to the user
- The importance to the survival of the organization.

Aspects of managing availability:

- Virus prevention and monitoring
- Business continuity planning
- Disaster recovery planning.

Security Policy

The primary driver of security in an IT environment is the security policy. To support the implementation of the security policies, mechanisms are installed, such as:

- Standards
- Procedures
- Guidelines
- Baselines.

Policies communicate management expectations. The policy creation practice should be clearly defined and cover:

- Initiation
- Creation
- Review

- Recommendation
- Approval
- Distribution.

Best practices for creating good security policies:

- Write policies that last two to three years
- Use directive wording
- Avoid technical implementation details
- Keep length to a minimum
- Provide links from policy to supporting documents
- Review details before publishing
- Conduct management review and sign-off
- Avoid technical language
- Adjust policies based on incident review
- Review policies regularly
- Develop noncompliance sanctions.

Security Policy Types:

- Organizational or program
- Functional, issue-specific
- System-specific.

Changes to policy will be more frequent when the policy is detailed. Therefore high level organizational polices may last several years, while system-specific policies would last for shorter timeframes as technologies mature and new technologies are added to the environment.

Standards

Policies define what an organization needs and standards define the minimum requirements for the organization.

Standards address hardware and software mechanisms to control security risks. They create agreements to ensure interoperability within the organization through common protocols.

Procedures

Procedures are detailed instructions to support the policies, standards, guidelines, and baselines. They indicate how to implement the policy and who performs the tasks required to fulfill the policy. They clarify the requirements of security and enable a common understanding of the operations required.

Development of procedures should involve all departments interfacing with the instructions. This is also beneficial to create a common understanding of the entire procedure by interacting organizations.

Baselines

Baselines ensure the implementation of security packages is consistent across the organization.

Baselines are impacted by differences in:

- Software packages
- Hardware platforms

- Networks
- Security methods
- Security options
- Security settings.

They are specific rules required to implement the security controls required to support the developed policies and standards. Testing of the security controls ensure the baselines are implemented appropriately.

Guidelines

Guidelines provide discretionary controls to enable individuals to make judgments in regards to providing better security.

Guidelines can consist of recommendations, best practices and templates created by the organization or provided by third party. Industry guidelines include:

- Control Objections for information and related Technology (COBIT)
- Capability Maturity Model (CMM)
- ISO 17799
- British Standard 7799
- National Institute of Standards and Technology (NIST)
- National Security Agency (NSA).

Audit Frameworks

Audits assist in the design of a security program by defining the necessary controls for securing information systems.

Several frameworks exist with varying focus:

- The Committee of Sponsoring Organizations of the Treadway Commission (COSO)
  Developed five areas of internal control for financial reporting and disclosure:
  - Control environmental
  - Risk assessments
  - Control activities
  - Information and communication
  - Monitoring
- IT Infrastructure Library
  34 books published within the Service Management discipline:
  - Service Strategy
  - Service Design
  - Service Transition
  - Service Operations
  - Continual Improvement
- Control Objectives for Information and related Technology (COBIT)
  34 high level processes and 214 control objectives modeled within four domains for governance:
  - Planning and organization

- Acquisition and implementation
- Delivery and supporting
- Monitoring

- BS 7799/ISO 17799

  Provides 134 information security controls in 11 areas:

  - Information security policies
  - Organizing information security
  - Asset Management
  - Human resources security
  - Physical and environmental security
  - Communications and operations management
  - Access control
  - Information systems acquisition, development, and maintenance
  - Information security incident management
  - Business continuity management
  - Compliance.

Security Organization

Though an organization may have a security department, security is the responsibility of everyone associated with the organization. The security department enforces the implementation and practice of security policies, standards and procedures.

Security concerns can be resolved through organizational processes and procedures, key personnel, reporting, oversight and planning.

Best Security Practices

Adoption of organizational best processes can protect the security of information, as well as identify areas of weakness in the organization:

Common best practices include:

- Job Rotation
- Separation of Duties
- Least Privileges
- Mandatory Vacations
- Job Position Sensitivity.

Job rotations allow for a reduction in collusion of activities and identifying activities which are outside the normal operating procedures.

Dividing the steps of a particular process ensures that a single individual doesn't have absolute control and knowledge of the process.

Granting access only for what is required to perform an individual's duty reduces the risk of inappropriate or unintended disclosure of information. Mandatory vacations provide similar benefits as rotating and separation of duties by providing opportunities to understanding the day-to-day performance of specific functions.

The access and duties of an individual can determine the sensitivity of the position and determine the level of control on security practices.

Information Security Officer

The responsibility for ensuring the protection of all business information assets from the loss, disclosure, alteration, destruction, and unavailability falls within the job scope of the Information Security Officer.

Primary duties include:

- Ensuring that security risks are appropriately communicated to executive management
- Establishing and managing a budget to conduct all information security activities
- Ensuring appropriate and timely development of security policies, procedures, baselines, standards, and guidelines
- Developing and providing a Security Awareness Program
- Ensuring the business objectives are understood and appropriately translated into security strategies
- Maintaining an awareness of emerging threats and vulnerabilities
- Evaluating security incidents and the response provided to identify strengths and weaknesses in security solutions
- Developing and enforcing a Security Compliance Program
- Establishing Metrics for Security Performance
- Conducting and participating in meetings with management to ensure that business concerns are appropriately addressed and communicated
- Ensuring compliance to government regulations
- Assisting in the auditing efforts from internal and external

departments
- Remaining current in emerging technologies.

Reporting

Responsibility for security implementations should fall to individuals at the highest levels of the organizations. Reporting to the highest levels assists in:

- Maintaining visibility of security solutions and needs
- Reducing the level of distortion or inaccuracies in reporting.

No organization model works best for all organizations from a security standpoint: however, some characteristics have been successful:

- Reporting to the CEO
- Reporting to the Information Technology (IT) Department
- Reporting to Corporate Security
- Reporting to the Administrative Services Department
- Reporting to the Insurance and Risk Management Department
- Reporting to the Internal Audit Department
- Reporting to the Legal Department.

In all cases, building credible and strong relations with executive management, middle management, and end users is a key factor in the success of the Information Security Office and the department he/she runs.

Security Council

Serves to align security objectives with business objectives. Actual responsibilities can be defined by the visions and mission statements of the Security Council.

The Security Council is comprised of management representatives from multiple organizations who are in a position to support the security policies.

While the information security department is responsible for implementing and enforcing security practices, the Security Council is responsible for recommending and approving security activities. Specific tasks for the Security Council can include:

- Deciding on project initiatives
- Prioritizing information security efforts
- Review and recommendation of security policies
- Promoting organizational security efforts
- Recommending investment areas.

Planning for Security

Planning for security should be holistic and involve:

- Strategic planning
- Tactical planning
- Project planning
- Operational planning.

Strategic planning specifically deals with aligning security plans with strategic business and information technology goals. They typically will provide a high-level, long-term perspective on security activities.

Tactical planning creates broad initiatives intended to support and achieve the strategic goals. Multiple projects may be conducted to fulfill the objectives derived from tactical planning.

Project planning is short term plans with specific milestones, dates, and accountabilities to communicate and direct activities to fulfill the strategic and tactical objectives of security planning. Project planning has clear start and end dates.

Operational planning is similar to project planning objectives without clear start and end dates. They typically involve recurring and repetitive ongoing tasks to maintain security presence.

Personnel

Security is the responsibility of all employees in the organization. As a result, how an organization treats its employees can impact the security position of the company, whether the employee is current, potential, or formal. Hiring and termination policies are key vulnerabilities for security.

When hiring individuals, several areas of focus can minimize security exposure:

- Clear job descriptions with detailed responsibilities and

requirements for education, experience and expertise

- Employment agreements to acknowledge legal and ethical responsibilities
- Checking on references with past employers
- Background checks, especially highly sensitive positions.

Background checks can cover a variety of searches into a person's past, including:

- Credit checks
- Criminal history
- Driving history
- Drug and substance testing
- Prior employment
- Verification of education, licensing, and certification
- Validation of social security listing
- Suspected terrorist watch list.

The level of background checking usually matches the security importance of the job position.

Periodic performance reviews and ongoing supervision is crucial to ensuring that security policies are being adopted properly from all employees in the organization.

Different levels of care are important considerations for handling terminations, especially related to whether they are friendly or unfriendly.

Education, Training, and Awareness

Security awareness is the understanding in the importance of security for the organization, the processes, and the customers. Security awareness training is a method of informing employees of their roles and related expectations as they relate to maintaining minimal information security requirements. In some cases, security awareness programs are a requirement for compliance to regulations, such as:

- HIPAA
- Sarbanes-Oxley Act
- Gram-Leach-Bliley Act.

Training and education may involve any combination of:

- Awareness activities
- Job training
- Professional training.

Performance metrics are a clear method of determining security needs and the effectiveness of training in the organization.

The architecture and design of the security solution must address the design, implementation, and operations of those controls used to enforce the levels of confidentiality, integrity, and availability required.

Security Components and Principles

System architectures are defined by three basic components:

- Central processing unit (CPU)

- Storage devices
- Peripherals.

Hardware Concepts

Mainframes are typically associated with centralized computing solutions while distributed environments are comprised of personal computers connected to a number of servers. Mainframes can run multiple operating systems and provide reliability, scalability, and maintainability with a lower total cost of ownership.

The business requirements will determine the system design required.

Another hardware consideration is within the realm of mobile computing, particularly personal digital assistants (PDA), Blackberry devices, iPhones and cell phones.

Central Process Unit (CPU)

Processing happens through the CPU by converting inputted raw data into useful output information. When the CPU requires data, it is retrieved from memory.

Several processing methods can be performed by the CPU to increase capabilities:

- Multitasking – the operating system switches from one process to the next to speed up processing
- Multiprocessing – simultaneous processing can be done

because of the existence of multiple CPUs

- Multithreading - threads are sliced and given to the CPU one at a time in an interleaved manner.

These capabilities can lead to some security vulnerabilities, namely protecting multiple processes from other processes which may contain bugs or unfriendly actions. A malicious process can assign or seize enough memory to create a DoS attack or crash the system.

Storage

Primary storage refers to the staging area for data waiting to be processed by the CPU. The location of the data is denoted by its physical memory address. Examples of primary storage include:

- ROM – read-only memory
- RAM – random access memory
- SDRAM – synchronous dynamic random-access memory.

Secondary storage holds the data not being used by the CPU. Computer systems use multiple media types which differ in storage capacity, access speed, access modes, and permanency of storage.

Virtual memory is an emulation of real memory, essentially extending the amount available to the user. Memory which is virtually created has greater flexibility and scalability than real memory. It allows more programs to run simultaneously.

Input/Output Devices

Computers receive raw information in the form of data. Programs are a collection of instructions for the computer.

In simplistic terms, input enters a device, process, or service. This input is processed using the instructions provided and creates an output.

The output is typically in the form of binary or hexadecimal notation and then translated into a format understood by the user.

Input devices provide the means to receive data, while output devices provide the means to give data in the form of text, video, images, and/or audio.

Input and output devices are controlled by small software programs called drivers. These drivers support the communication channels used for system I/O. The communication channel of the I/O device will provide different interfaces for different signals within its limitations.

Networks

Networks bind computer systems and services together across a site. This allows users to share resources and exchange data. Local Area Networks are a connection of local computer systems.

Wide Area Networks typically connect several LANs together into a larger collection of networks. The Internet is a loose connection of wide area networks.

Each network can have different policies that are applied to control and define who can access, what can be accessed, how that access looks, and when the resources are available. Individual networks can be partitioned, or segmented, to allow greater ability to manage policies, including greater restrictive permissions.

Software

Software is a set of instructions performed by the CPU to obtain a specific result. There are three types of programs:

- Operating systems
- Programming languages
- Middleware and applications.

Operating Systems

Operating systems control the general operation of the computer, as well as the input and output between peripherals. In multiuser systems, operating systems will manage the user access.

At the core of the operating system is the kernel, which allows access to system resources. The system kernel is responsible for:

- Supplying vital services
- Executing binary programs
- Scheduling task swapping
- Allocating memory

- Tracking the physical location of files.

The kernel acts as an intermediary between programs under its controls and the physical hardware of the computer. The kernel can determine invalid requests between the programs and hardware and act appropriately.

A security kernel is the hardware, firmware, and software components of a trusted computing base. It mediates all access.

The CPU has two states: supervisor state and problem state. The supervisor state, or kernel mode, the CPU operates at the highest possible privilege on the system allowing access to any and all system resources.

Applications run in a problem state, or user mode, and have limited access to system data and hardware.

When the operating system is managing the resources available to the computer and processing information, it is in supervisor mode. When it is running applications, the operating system switches to problem mode.

Application Programs

Applications perform specific functions around a set of instructions. The functions are different based on the type of applications; however, the general processing remains the same.

When an application executes, it spawns a process or instance of the program. The process will request the resources it needs, which are called handles or descriptors.

The operating system will allocate the required resources to the program, allowing the process to move through its various stages until it is complete.

When a process requests resources, it creates one or more independent threads. Threads can be created by other threads or be joined with other threads. They have different attributes and options. Threads are either running or waiting to run.

Threads are really lightweight processes, but they are easier to create than a full fledged program. Multiple threads share everything which reduces the overhead costs of running them.

There are two drawbacks to using threads:

- Deadlocks
- Blocking.

Middleware is connectivity software which allows multiple processes running on one or more machines to interact. Used in distributed environments, middleware allows seamless integration of network technologies, computer architectures, operating systems and programming languages.

Other Software

Firmware is embedded into hardware for the purposes of controlling that hardware. It is a set of instructions usually found in erasable programmable read-only memory (EEPROM). Firmware is upgradeable.

The Trusted Computed Base (TCB) is a combination of hardware, firmware, and software enforcing the security processes. The mechanisms associated to the TCB work with the administration information provided by the system support. The TCB is defined by the Department of Defense Trusted Computer System Evaluation Criteria or Orange Book for short.

The reference monitor is an abstract machine mediating all access to objects.

Security Models

Security policies are formally described using security models. An organization's security policy documents the requirements of the organization and becomes a guide for defending against security threats and mitigating risk.

A security model, or access control model, implements the rules of the security policy.

Access Control Models

Four access control models exist:

- State machine model - operating system is allowed to transition between well-defined states
- Access matrix model – a combination of read, write, and execute permissions are assigned to users. Within the matrix, the users are represented by rows and resources are represented by columns
- Take-grant model – illustrates using graphs the security permissions taken and granted between objects
- Bell-LaPadua model – a lattice-based model designed to enforce the military's Mandatory Access Control (MAC) mode with two rules:
    - Simple security rule - information can only flow from lower levels of security to higher levels
    - Property rule - users can never write information to a lower clearance level.

Integrity Models

Two integrity models exist:

- Biba model - a lattice-based model complementing the Bell-LaPadua model with two rules:
    - Simple integrity axiom – information cannot be written to higher security levels
    - Integrity axiom – information at a lower security cannot be read by a user with higher levels

- Clark-Wilson model – maintains data integrity by enforcing a separation of duty.

Rainbow Series

A series of books published in 1985 by the National Computer Security Center. The books are called the Rainbow Series because each one can be identified by the color of their covers:

- Orange Book – includes the DoD Trusted Computer System Evaluation Criteria (TCSEC)
- Red Book – the Trusted Network Interpretation of the TCSEC
- Purple Book – the DoD Trusted Database Management System
- Green Book – the DoD Password Management Guideline
- Amber Book – the Guide to Understanding Configuration Management in Trusted System.

The Trusted Computer System Evaluation Criteria (TCSEC) specifies criteria for evaluation systems:

- A set of laws, rules, and practices, called the security policy, must be available to describe how to regulate how an organization manages, protects, and distributes sensitive information
- Each user of a trusted system must be uniquely identified
- Each security object must be labeled to describe the sensitivity of the object

- The compliance of a trusted system to TCSEC criteria must be completely documented
- User actions must be auditable at an individually identifiable level
- Formal methods should be used to validate the system design and implementation processes
- The trusted computing system must be continuously protected against unauthorized changes.

Specific designations are awarded under TCSEC as follows:

- Minimal Protection (D) systems have been evaluated but fail to meet the requirements for a higher evaluation criteria
- Discretionary Protection (C1)systems satisfy the criteria for discretionary access controls including:
    - Identification and Authentication
    - Discretionary Access Control Security Policy
    - Operational Assurance of System Architecture and System Integrity
    - Lifecycle Assurance of Security Testing
    - Proper documentation for:
        - Security Features Users' Guide
        - Trusted Facility Manual
        - Test Documentation
        - Design Documentation
- Controlled Access Protection (C2) systems build on C1 requirements to have more granular discretionary access controls:

- Object Reuse Security Policy
- Auditing procedures

- Labeled Security Protection (B1) systems meet C2 systems requirements and introduce labeling requirements such as:
  - Label Integrity Policy
  - Policy on exportation of Labeled Information to Single-Level Devices, MultiLevel Devices, and Human-Readable Output
  - Mandatory Access Control Policy
  - Lifecycle Assurance of Design Specification and Verification
- Structured Protection (B2) systems build on B1 requirements making them relatively resistant to penetration:
  - Addresses Subject Sensitivity Labels and Device Labels in the Labeling Policy
  - Trusted Path for Identification and Authentication
  - Adds to the Operational Assurance of Covert Channel Analysis
  - Adds to the Trusted Facility Management
  - Configuration Management of Lifecycle Assurance
- Security Domains (B3) systems are highly resistant to penetration and builds on B2 requirements, adding:
  - Trusted Recovery Operational Assurance
  - Uses a Trusted Computing Base (TCB) to allow rigorous testing

- Verified Design (A1) systems do not add any requirements or features: certification is granted because formal techniques for design specification and verification are in place.

The techniques used by A1 systems follow a five step process:

- Development of a formal model of the security policy which includes mathematical proof
- Development of a formal top-level specification (FTLS) of the design including definitions of functions
- Formal and informal techniques used to verify the FTLS is consistent with the model
- Verify the implementation of the TCB is consistent with the FTLS through informal techniques
- Formal analysis performed to identify any covert channels in the system.

Information Technology Security Evaluation Criteria (ITSEC)

The ITSEC is used in Europe and addresses confidentiality, integrity, and availability. The criteria results in two ratings: functionality (F1-F10) and assurance (E0-E6).

ITSEC maps to and extends the TCSEC.

Common Criteria

Described by ISO/IEC15408, the Common Criteria for Information

Technology Security Evaluation (CC) was developed with the cooperation of several governments. The Common Criteria model replaces:

- The U.S. Trusted Computer System Evaluation Criteria (TCSEC)
- The European Information Technology Security Evaluation Criteria (ITSEC)
- The Canadian Trusted Computer Product Evaluation Criteria (CTCPEC).

The model defines the use of:

- Protection profiles – product's security requirements
- Security targets – vendor's design claims for a structured system to evaluate IT products.

The evaluation of products results in the assignment of an Evaluation Assurance Level (EAL):

- EAL1 – functionally tested
- EAL2 – structurally tested
- EAL3 – methodically tested and checked
- EAL4 – methodically designed, tested and reviewed
- EAL5 – semiformally designed and tested
- EAL6 – semiformally verified design and tested
- EAL7 – formally verified design and tested.

Certification and Accreditation

Security professionals define distinct processes for certification and accreditation. Specific definitions provided by the U.S. Department of Defense are:

- Accreditation is a formal declaration by the Designated Accrediting Authority (DAA) that shows an IT system is approved to operate in a particular security mode with a set of prescribed safeguards used at an acceptable level of risk
- Certification provides a comprehensive evaluation of technical and non-technical security features of an IT system and safeguard to determine to a particular design or implementation meets specified security requirements.

Physical Network Topologies

Networks utilize physical devices. They are also connected physically. How they are connected is based on their requirements and the needs of the organization. Several possible topologies may be considered including:

- Star
- Mesh
- Bus
- Ring
- Point-to-Point
- Point-to-Multipoint
- Hybrid.

Star

In the star topology, each host on the network segment is connected to a central hub though a point-to-point connection. The hub will act as a repeater or signal booster. It is the easiest topology to design and implement. Adding machines to the network requires a simple connection to the hub. Unfortunately, the hub becomes a single point of failure for the network.

Two special versions of the star topology are the extended and distributed star. Within an extended star network, any spoke of the star can be extended using a repeater in order to increase the maximum transmission distance of the link. If the repeater is replaced with a hub, a hybrid topology is created commonly referred to as a physical hierarchical star topology. In a distributed star topology, individual networks are connected together in a linear fashion.

Mesh

The most complicated network topology is the meshed network. In this type of network, all hosts on the network are connected to every other host on the network. This is also the most expensive network topology to design and implement, though it provides the greatest level of reliability and availability.

Two classifications of the mesh topology exist: fully connected and partially connected. In a fully connected topology, each node has a point-to-point connection with every node on the network segment. This allows data to be simultaneously transmitted to all other nodes on the network. In a partially connected mesh, some of the nodes are connected to more than one other node in the network using a point-to-point link. This form allows the redundancy of mesh networking without the extreme costs or complexity.

Bus

The bus topology refers to the network design where several hosts are connected to a single cable with a terminator at each end. When data is sent from one host it travels in both directions along the bus cable until it reaches its destination. The terminator prevents the signal from bouncing back. This is the most inexpensive network to implement, but the bus cable becomes the single point of failure.

A bus topology can be linear or distributed. In a linear bus network, all the nodes are connected to a single cable with exactly two endpoints. The cable or transmission medium is referred to as the trunk or backbone. In a distributed bus network the nodes are connected to a common transmission medium which has more than two endpoints. This is caused because branches off the primary section are created, but functions just like a linear bus topology.

Ring

In a ring topology, each node on the network is connected to two of its neighbors in opposite directions, until all nodes are connected in a closed loop, or ring. The most commonly known ring network is IBM's Token Ring. When a node transmits on the network, the data is sent in one direction, hitting each node on the network until its destination is reached. A token is typically used to control access to the network. In this scheme only one machine can transmit at a time. All other nodes act as repeaters or signal boosters for the transmission. Unfortunately in this network, if one node fails the entire network fails.

Point-to-Point

Point-to-point topologies are a link between two endpoints. A permanent link provides a guaranteed communication between the two points. In circuit-switched or packet-switched networks, a point-to-point circuit is created dynamically and temporarily and remains in place until it is not longer required.

Following the same concept, the point-to-multipoint topology allows a single node to broadcast or multicast to multiple hosts on the network. The connections are made with the requesting host as the central point and any single connection can end whenever it is not required. Additional connections can be made at any time.

Hybrid

Hybrids are any combination of the same topology or different topologies connected together. For instance, a bus topology can create a backbone for an organization where all departments are connected together. The physical network for each department is a star topology where the hub is connected as a node on the backbone.

Logical Network Topologies

Peer-To-Peer Networks

Peer-to-Peer networks have no hierarchy of computers. Each computer on the network can act as a server or a client. Each user is responsible for the security and sharing functions of their individual computers. The networks are limited to 15-20 computers. The most popular operating systems supporting P2P networks are:

- Microsoft Windows for Workgroups
- Microsoft Windows 2000
- Novell's Netware
- UNIX
- Linux.

Server/Client Networks

Server/Client networks consist of one or more dedicated computers used as servers. The servers manage the access to all shared files and peripherals. Network Operating Systems (NOS) manages security and provides access administration to resources. Clients on the network use the resources available by the servers. Common operating systems supporting Server/Client networks:

- Microsoft Windows NT Server 4
- Microsoft Windows 2000
- Novell's Netware.

IPSec

When two hosts want to communicate securely over an untrusted network, they can use an encrypted tunnel called a Virtual Private Network (VPN). This is a popular solution for remote users, but also to mask the IP address of individual computers usually to browse the Web anonymously. The links between nodes are formed over logical connections or virtual circuits between hosts of the larger network.

VPNs utilize a suite of protocols, called IP Security (IPSec), to communicate securely using IP. IPSec provides mechanisms for authentication and encryption. Standard IPSec will only authenticate hosts with each other. Organizations must deploy a nonstandard proprietary IPSec implementation, or use L2TP (Layer 2 Tunneling Protocol) to encapsulate IPSec packets within.

The authentication header (AH) plays an important part in ensuring that the packet has not been tampered with. The AH ensures the integrity of the packet, not the confidentiality.

Confidentiality is aided by the encapsulated security payload (ESP) which encrypts IP packets and ensures integrity. Both services are optional, though one must be used. ESP contains four sections:

- ESP header – contains information about security association and sequence number
- ESP payload – the encrypted part of the packet
- ESP trailer – padding required by encryption algorithm
- Authentication – a field containing the integrity check value

(hash).

Security associations (SA) define the mechanisms used by an endpoint to communicate. They cover one-way transmissions only. To communicate in the opposite direction, a second SA must be used.

To communicate with IPSec, endpoints use either transport or tunnel mode. Transport mode protects the IP payload only, while tunnel mode protects both the payload and IP header. Tunnel mode is typically found in transmissions between networks.

LAN Technologies

LAN Properties

Networks have to deal with collision, but have the means to determine if and when a collision happens. This is possible because of a protocol called Carrier Sense Multiple Access / Collision Detection (CSMA/CD). Since collisions cannot be detected on wireless LANs effectively, the best option is to avoid them. A similar protocol is CSMA/CA (CA stands for Collision Avoidance) was created for this purpose. The primary difference between the two protocols is the dependence of positive acknowledgments (ACKs) for CSMA/CA.

Collision is an isolated event where two or more data packets exert force against each other within a very short time frame. In networking, CSMA/CD is a method where the transmitting device will stop transmitting the next frame when another signal is detected. In addition, it will transmit a jam signal and wait for a random time interval before sending the frame it intended to transmit. The methods used for collision detection are dependent on the media.

Both collision detection and collision avoidance are modifications to CSMA, which is used to verify the presence or absence of traffic on a shared transmission medium. There are three types of CSMA:

- 1-persistent CSMA – checks if the medium is busy and if so, will continually sense until idle
- p-persistent CSMA – checks the medium continually until it is idle
- Nonpersistent CSMA – checks if the medium is busy and if so, will wait a period of time before checking again.

On a wired network, the overhead attributed to CSMA/CD on an average use network is about 30%. When the wired network becomes congested, the overhead can increase to 70%. A wireless network will remain at a constant 50-55% throughput when congested.

Broadcasting is the concept of a transmitted packet being received by every device on the network. Not all computer networks will support broadcasting, which is done mostly on LANs. The extent of the broadcast can be controlled using routers and other filtering devices between network segments. Ethernet and IPv4 networks utilize a broadcast address to indicate broadcast packets.

Ethernet

Network technologies are used to establish network connectivity, and the most popular technology is Ethernet, because of its low cost, scalability, and availability. Ethernet is based on the Institute of Electrical and Electronic Engineers (IEEE) 802.3 standard and offers 10 Mbps bandwidth between hosts.

Cabling is a major enabler of Ethernet with coaxial cabling being the first media system of the standard. Coaxial categories include Thicknet (10Base5) and Thinnet (10Base2). The differences are in size and length limitations. Thicknet has a diameter of 5mm and length of 500m while thinnet has a diameter of 10mm and length of 185m. Cables are susceptible to electromagnetic interference (EMI) and eavesdropping.

Twisted-pair media are prevalent for desktop connectivity. Twisted-pair are one pair of insulated copper wires twisted about each other. Categories include: unshielded twisted-pair (UTP) and shielded twisted-pair (STP). The twisting of the wires reduces interference and crosstalk. These cables are restricted to 100 meters between active devices due to risk of high attenuation. They are also sensitive to EMI and eavesdropping. Most networks use 10BaseT UTP cabling.

Fiber optic cables (10BaseFL) transmit light signals. These light signals can be generated using light emitting diodes (LED) or laser diodes (LD) and support higher transmission speeds and longer distances. Fiber optics are very expensive to implement and immune to EMI and eavesdropping. Low attenuation with fiber options allows 2km distance between active devices.

Fast Ethernet is based on the IEEE 802.3u standard and operates at 100 Mbps. It is compatible with the slower Ethernet because the two devices automatically negotiate link capabilities in order to work at a common level. Negotiation detects and selects the highest available bandwidth and operations at half-duplex or full-duplex. Fast Ethernet is also known as 10/100 Mbps Ethernet. Its cabling solution is either UTP or fiber optic.

Technology	**Type of Wire**	**Pairs**	**Cable Length**
100BaseTX	EIA/TIA Category 5 UTP	2	100 m
100BaseT2	EIA/TIA Category 3,4,5 UTP	2	100 m
100BaseT4	EIA/TIA Category 3,4,5 UTP	4	100 m
100BaseFX	Multimode fiber (MMF) with 62.5 micron core; 1300 nm laser Single-mode fiber (SMF) with 62.5 micron core; 1300 nm laser	1	400 m (half-duplex) 2000 m (full-duplex)

Gigabit Ethernet is based on IEEE 802.3 and American National Standards Institute (ANSI) X3T11 FibreChannel or combined as IEEE 802.3z Gigabit Ethernet. It operates at 1000 Mbps (1 Gbps) and is compatible with other Ethernet standards. A modified physical layer increases data transmission speeds. IEEE 802.3 provides frame format, CSMA/CD, full duplex and other Ethernet characteristics. FiberChannel provides high-speed AISC, optical components, and mechanisms for encoding, decoding, and serialization.

100-Gigabit Ethernet is also found.

Technology	Type of Wire	Pairs	Cable Length
1000BaseCX	Shielded Twisted Pair (STP)	1	25 m
1000BaseT	EIA/TIA Category 3,4,5 UTP	4	100 m
1000BaseSX	Multimode fiber (MMF) with 62.5 micron core; 850 nm laser Multimode fiber (MMF) with 62.5 micron core; 1300 nm laser	1 1	275 m 550 m
1000BaseLX/LH	Multimode fiber (MMF) with 62.5 micron core; 1300 nm laser Single-mode fiber (SMF) with 62.5 micron core; 1300 nm laser Single-mode fiber (SMF) with 62.5 micron core; 1300 nm laser	1 1 1	550 m 550 m 10 km
1000BaseZX	Single-mode fiber (SMF) with 62.5 micron core; 1550 nm laser Single-mode fiber (SMF) with 62.5 micron core; 1550 nm laser	1 1	70 km 100 km

10GBaseSR	Multimode fiber (MMF)	1	26 – 82 m
10GBaseLR	Single-mode fiber (SMF)	1	10 km
10GBaseER	Single-mode fiber (SMF)	1	40 km
10GBaseSW	Uses WAN PHY to interoperated with OC-192/STM-64 SONET/SDG	1	26 – 82 m
10GBaseLW	Uses WAN PHY to interoperated with OC-192/STM-64 SONET/SDG	1	10 km
10GBaseEW	Uses WAN PHY to interoperated with OC-192/STM-64 SONET/SDG	1	40 km
10DBaseT			

Networking Features

Power over Ethernet (PoE) Devices

When AC power receptacles are not available to power a unit, wireless devices can receive DC power over a Cat5 Ethernet cable. The method is called Power of Ethernet (PoE). The cable used will carry both power and data to the unit. This is done with a POE device on the cable line. Cable requirements related to data transfer still apply, namely that Ethernet cables can only carry data reliably for 100 meters. PoE has such great advantages that some manufacturers build devices that will only use PoE.

Several types of PoE devices exist, including:

- Single-port DC voltage injectors

- Multi-port Voltage injectors
- Ethernet switches designed to inject DC voltage.

Configuration and management is not necessary for a PoE device, though some considerations must be known. No industry standard exists for the implementation of PoE: which generally prevent how PoE equipment interfaces with other devices. Therefore, if you are using a PoE device to power an access point, it is best to use devices from the same manufacturer.

The output voltage required to power a wireless LAN will be different form one manufacturer to the next. Using devices from the same manufacturer will mitigate any compatibility issues. The current that is carried over Ethernet utilizes unused pins that are not standardized. One manufacturer may use pins 7 and 8 while another uses 4 and 5. If a wireless LAN device does not accept power on those pins, the device will not power up.

Using Power-over-Ethernet requires the use of an injector. If the wireless device is PoE compatible, no other equipment is required. If the device is not PoE compatible, a picker is required.

Single-port DC voltage injectors are used to power wireless LAN devices. They are specifically used when the use of PoE is mandatory for the access point or bridge. Single-port injectors should only be used in small networks to prevent clutter. For medium sized networks, a multi-port injector will support the power requirements for several devices, typically manufactured to have 4, 6, or 12 output ports. The

PoE device is typically sitting within a wiring closet and connected to a switch or hub on the input port and the wireless devices on the output ports. Up to 50 access points can be supported.

Large sized networks would benefit from the installation of active Ethernet switches. The device incorporates DC voltage injections into the Ethernet switch. The benefit is the support of large numbers of PoE devices without additional hardware. In most cases, an active Ethernet switch can auto-detect any PoE requirements on the network. If PoE is not required, than the DC voltage is switched off on the connecting port.

Injectors come in two types:

- Passive
- Fault protected.

A passive injector simply places a DC voltage onto a Cat5 cable.

A fault protected injectors also places a DC voltage on a Cat5 cable, but also provides continuous fault monitoring and protection to detect short circuits and over-current conditions.

Devices that are not designed to use PoE can be converted using a DC “picker” or “tap.” Also called active Ethernet “splitters,” these devices siphon the DC voltage that was injected in the Cat5 cable by the injector and make it available to the non-PoE device through a regular DC power jack.

Pickers come in two types:

- Passive
- Regulated.

A passive picker will take the voltage from the Cat5 cable and direct it to the equipment. Therefore, the equipment will receive whatever VDS (Volts of Direct Current) were originally injected.

A regulated tap will take the voltage from the Cat5 cable and convert it to another voltage, typically standard regulated voltages of 5 VDC, 6 VDC, and 12 VDC.

The injected PoE voltage has been standardized at 48 VDC by the IEEE. However, higher voltage will reduce the current flowing through the Cat5 cable. This will cause the load to increase and the limitations on the length of the Cat5 cable. Some manufacturers have decided to utilize 12 or 24 VDC.

Fault protection is meant to protect the cable equipment and power supply from short-circuit or fault. Under normal operations, faults are highly unexpected; though several causes may contribute:

- Incompatibility with PoE
- Non-standard or defective connectors
- Incorrectly wired Cat5 cabling
- Cut or crushed Cat5 cabling.

Fault protection will shut DC voltage off whenever a fault condition exists.

Circuit operation varies from one model to the next. Restoring power is dependent on the device model. Some models will continuously monitor the cable and automatically restore power when the fault has been resolved. Other models must be manually reset.

Spanning-Tree Protocol (STP)

The Spanning-Tree Protocol allows redundant LAN links while preventing frames from looping around the LAN. It was developed to overcome the possibility of bridging loops by enabling switches to know about other switches on the network. This knowledge of switches enables the ability to negotiate a loop-free path. Loops within the network are discovered and redundant links are shut down

STP is communicated to all switches on the network and computes a tree structure that covers all switches within the network. Each switch will execute the Spanning Tree Algorithm (STA) which chooses a reference point and calculates all redundant paths. When redundant paths are found, STA will pick one path and block all other paths. If forwarding fails, the STA will recompute the Spanning-Tree topology.

By default, STP is enabled on all ports, and STP should remain enabled.

STP has three criteria to determine to put an interface in the forwarding state:

- Elects a root bridge and puts all interfaces on the root bridge in forwarding state
- Places the lowest-root-cost interface, or root port, in forwarding state
- Lowest cost bridge, or designation bridge, and that bridge's interface , or designated port.

All other interfaces are placed in blocking state. Low cost means lowest administrative cost between two points.

The Spanning-Tree Protocol creates a Root Bridge as a common reference point for all switches in a network. A common reference point is required to allow a loop-free topology and a Root Bridge is chosen by election.

Each switch has a unique Bridge ID used to identify itself to other switches. The bridge ID is an 8-byte value: 2 bytes identify priority, remaining 6 for the MAC Address. The priority is relative to all other switches on the network. The MAC Address is derived from the Supervisor module, the backplane, or a pool of 1024 addresses that are assigned to every Supervisor or backplane based on switch model. The MAC address is hardcoded, unique, and cannot be changed.

The election process proceeds as follows:

1. Every switch sends out BPDUs with a Root Bridge ID and a Sender Bridge ID.
2. The Root Bridge ID must be equal to its own Bridge ID.

3. The Sender Bridge ID is used to identify the source of the BPDU.
4. Received BPDU messages are analyzed for a lower Root Bridge ID value.
5. The Root Bridge ID from the received message and the switch are compared.
6. If the message's Root Bridge ID is the lowest, it replaces the switch's Root Bridge ID.
7. If the two are equal, than the MAC addresses are compared and the lowest is chosen.
8. The new Root Bridge ID becomes part of the switch's BPDU message as a nomination.
9. Eventually, all switches will agree on the Root Bridge until a new switch is added.

The election process is based on the idea that a common reference point and all switches choose ports closest to the Root. Theoretically, the Root Bridge is the central hub that interconnects other legs of the network. The Root Bridge can be faced with heavy switching loads, so the slowest switch is not the best candidate. There is only one Root Bridge which is not fault tolerant. A secondary Root Bridge can be established in case the primary Root Bridge failed. The primary and secondary Root Bridges should be placed at the center of the network.

Once a Root Bridge is established, each non-root switch must find its relation to the Root Bridge. This relation is established by identifying the Root Port. The Root Path Cost is used to select the Root Port and is the cumulative cost of all links to the Root Bridge. Cost is associated with each switch link, called a Port or Path Cost. The Root Path Cost determines two things: its relationship to the Root Bridge and which port is the closest to the root.

The process of determining the Root Path Cost is:

1. Root Bridge sends out a BPDU with a Root Path Cost.
2. The value of the Root Path Cost is 0.
3. The BPDU is received by the next switch where its Path Cost is added to the Root Path Cost.
4. The new Root Path Cost is stored in memory of the current Switch.
5. The BPDU is sent out from this switch.
6. As the process continues, BPDUs may be received by multiple ports on a switch; the lowest Root Path Cost is stored in memory.
7. This process continues until each switch has a stored Root Path Cost.

The value of a port can be modified to influence the election of the Root Port.

After determining the Root Bridge and the Root Paths, each switch still has active links to other switches, creating possible bridging loops. To remove bridging loops, STP identifies one designated port on each network segment where traffic is routed. The designated port is based on the Root Path Cost.

Each port of a switch will go through several states when using STP. The ports states are:

- Blocking – No forwarding, BPDUs received
- Listening – Frames received, but not forwarded
- Learning – Addresses learned but frames are not forwarded
- Forwarding – Addresses learned and frames are forwarded
- Disabled – No forwarding, no BPDUs received.

Bridge Protocol Data Units (BPDUs) take a finite amount of time to travel from switch to switch. When topology changes are made, delays may occur as the new change is communicated to the entire network. STP has three timers:

- Hello Time – time interval between configuration BPDUs.
- Forward Delay – time interval that a switch port spends in both Listening and Learning states. Default value is 15 seconds.
- Max Age – time interval that a switch stores a BPDU before discarding it.

Timers can only be modified on the Root Bridge.

Trunking

Trunking is a concept in communications where a system can provide access to the network to many clients by sharing a set of lines or frequencies instead of providing them individually. A trunk is a single transmission channel between two points; one point being the switching center and the other, the node. Trunking is performed when multiple network cables or ports are used in parallel to increase the link speed being the limitations of a single cable or port. This process is called port trunking or link aggregation.

VLANs use trunking to carry multiple VLANs through a single network link. It is required when multiple interconnected switches are in use

A trunk line can allow more than one VLAN through a port. It is not assigned to a specific VLAN. The trunk line allows connecting two switches with separate physical links for each VLAN and supports multiple VLANs with members on more than one switch.

Two trunking protocols available on switches (namely Cisco):

- Inter-Switch Link (ISL)
- IEEE 802.1Q

The Inter-Switch Link (ISL) is one of the first trunking protocols and Cisco proprietary. It can be used between two Cisco switches only. ISL encapsulates each Ethernet frame in an ISL header and trailer without changing the frame. ISL headers include a VLAN field to encode the VLAN number to ensure the receiving switch knows which VLAN the frame belongs to. The source and destination addresses in the ISL header communicate the MAC addresses of the sending and receiving switch.

IEEE 802.1Q does not encapsulate like ISL but adds a 4-byte header to the original Ethernet header. It includes a field for the VLAN number. Because the original header is changed, a recalculation of the original FCS field is forced.

IEEE 802.1Q introduces the concept of a native VLAN on a trunk. Frames with this VLAN are not encapsulated with tagging information. Hosts can only receive and understand native VLAN frames.

Port Mirroring

Port Mirroring will send identical copies of the same network packets to two switch ports for the specific purpose of network monitoring. It is especially useful for diagnostic or debugging purposes. An administrator can keep close track of the traffic over a switch and its performance and make adjustments when necessary. This can be done locally or from a remote location.

Some switches support only one-to-one port mirroring meaning that only one port can be monitored. Other devices will support mirroring several ports into one destination port.

Port Authentication

IEEE 802.1x standards stipulate methods for restricting access to networks using authentication information, specifically port authentication. With this concept, a network controller can restrict external devices from accessing the network behind an 802.1x controlled port. Port access control is enabled by making devices attached to a controlled port to authenticate themselves through an authentication server before allowing access.

There are three components to 802.1x implementation:

- An authenticator – a port that enforces authentication before allowing access to services
- A supplicant – the port that wants to access services offered by the authenticating system
- An authentication server – a device that uses the authentication credentials supplied by the supplicant to the authenticator to determine whether access should be provided.

Virtual LANs

Virtual LANs are a flat network topology creating a single broadcast domain and act as a fully Layer 2 switched network. The more hosts in the network, the more broadcasts domains. Redundancies for load balancing and fault tolerance are not available.

Virtual LANs (VLANs) allow switched network to be subdivided into logical groupings. Each subdivided network becomes a single broadcast domain. All devices connected to a VLAN receive broadcasts from other devices on the VLAN and broadcasts from other VLANs are not received.

Members of the VLAN can be connected anywhere in the network as long as connectivity is provided. Layer 2 switches have VLAN mappings and will provide logical connectivity.

End-users must be able to gain membership to a VLAN and can do so through two methods: static VLANs and dynamic VLANs.

Static VLANs offer port-based membership. Switch ports are assigned to specific VLANs. End devices will automatically assume VLAN connectivity when a port is connected. No handshaking or unique VLAN membership protocol needed. Membership is handled by hardware with application specific integrated circuits (ASICs) in the switch. Static VLANs provide good performance because all port mappings are done at the hardware level.

Dynamic VLANs provide membership based on MAC address. This allows the greatest flexibility and mobility, but requires more administrative overhead. When connected, a device must query a database to establish membership. A network administrator will assign a MAC address to a VLAN in the VLAN Membership Policy Server (VPS) database.

The number of VLANs implemented is influenced by:

- Traffic patterns
- Application types
- Common workgroup segmentation
- Network management requirements
- Relationship between VLANs and IP addressing schemes.

VLANs can be scaled in the switch block using: end-to-end VLANs and local VLANs. End-to-end VLANs span the entire switch fabric and are also know as campus-wide VLANs. They support maximum flexibility and mobility of end devices. Users connecting to the networks are assigned regardless of physical location.

Local VLANs enable access to central resources outside their VLANs. Typically, more traffic goes through the network core. It is designed to contain user communities by geography, regardless of traffic leaving the VLAN. The size of the VLAN ranges from a single switch to entire buildings.

Virtual Private Networks (VPNs)

Where VLANs partition physical LANs to create virtual LANs, VPNs are multiple remote end-points which are joined using a tunnel over another network. Commonly found connecting two points over the Internet, VPNs provide a secure means of communicating data between gateways of software clients.

Basic Terms

The following terms are used in secure VPN implementations:

- VPN – a private network configured with a public network
- VPN Tunnel – an exclusive channel or encrypted link between gateways
- VPN topology – a collection of links that show the layout of the VPN. Typically are mesh or star network topologies
- VPN gateway – an endpoint for an encrypted connection which can consist of a single standalone module or cluster

of modules

- VPN domain – a grouping of hosts or networks for which encryption of the IP datagram is performed. A VPN gateway serves as an entry point for a VPN domain
- Site to Site VPN – the VPN tunnel between gateways
- Remote Access VPN – a VPN tunnel between remote users accessing the network with client software and gateways
- Encryption algorithm – a set of processes for rendering information into a meaningless format that has been mathematically transformed and converted using a special key
- Integrity – the provision of integrity checks using hash functions ensure a message has not been intercepted or altered during transmission
- Trust – established between gateways using a Public Key Infrastructure (PKI), certificates, and certificate authorities
- IKE and IPSec – VPN protocols used to manage encryption keys and exchange encrypted packets. IPSec is an encryption technology framework supporting several standards for authenticating and encrypting data services on a private or public network. Internet Key Exchange is a key management protocol standard which enhances IPSec through additional features, flexibility, and easier configuration.

Site to Site VPN

The encrypted tunnel or VPN link is the basic logical component of Virtual Private Networks. It is created using the IKE and IPSec protocols. It establishes a connection between two parties, either VPN-1 Power gateways or remote access clients. To establish a link, the two parties will create trust through certificate authorities, PKI, or a pre-shared secret. During this trust building, methods are exchanged and keys are created. The result is an encrypted tunnel that can be maintained for multiple connections. A single gateway can maintain multiple tunnels simultaneously with its peers. Traffic in a tunnel is encrypted and authenticated between VPN peers to ensure integrity and confidentiality.

VPN Communities

The two network topologies commonly used are mesh and star. A topology, in the context of VPNs, is a collection of enabled VPN links within a system of gateways, VPN domains, hosts internal to the gateways, and remote users external to the gateways. This collection or topology forms the VPN community.

In a mesh community, every gateway has an established link with every other gateway. In a star community, a central gateway, or hub, manages the communications of the entire network. Other gateways are considered satellites, or spokes, which communicate to the hub, but not each other directly. The layout of the mesh and star topologies can be expanded to provide greater capabilities.

Terms used within the VPN Community concept include:

- VPN Community Member
- VPN Domain
- VPN Site
- VPN Community
- Domain Based VPN
- Route Based VPN.

Remote Access VPN

Accessing a network using remote access must follow two sets of requirements: the basic requirements for accessing a network, plus the added requirements based on the special demands of remote access.

Remote users can securely communicate sensitive information to networks and services over a VPN tunnel, using dial-up (broadband), LAN, and wireless LAN connections. Either the internal database of the VPN-1 Power gateway or an external LDAP server can be used to manage remote users.

IPSec and IKE

Symmetric cryptography systems have both parties using the same key for encryption and decryption of information. The components of these keys must be exchanged between the two parties in a secure manner and must remain exclusive to the two parties. Internet Key Exchange (IKE) is designed to allow both sides to independently produce the same symmetrical key. It builds a VPN tunnel by authenticating both ends and negotiating an agreement on the methods for encryption and integrity. The intended results of an IKE negotiation is an established Security Association (SA).

Diffie-Hellman (DH) is a part of the IKE protocol for exchanging the components of the symmetrical keys used. The DH algorithm builds an encryption key from the private key of one endpoint and the public key of the second endpoint, creating a shared secret between the two endpoints.

The IKE Process

The IKE Process is composed of two phases. The first phase sets the foundation for the second phase. In the first phase:

- Peers authenticate using certificates or a pre-shared secret
- A DH key is created
- Keys and methods are exchanged and/or negotiated between peers.

The security association is now established for use in the second phase. The creation of the DH key is slow and requires lots of computations, causing a decrease in performance.

The second phase focuses on exchanging materials between peers to build the IPSec keys, which results in the establishment of the IPSec Security Association.

Methods of Encryption and Integrity

Negotiation in both phases of the process set the parameters for the:

- Encryption Algorithm
- Hash Algorithm.

The encryption algorithms negotiated in the first phase (IKE SA) are AES-256 (default), 3DES, DES, and CAST. The second phase (IPSec SA) will negotiate 3DEA, AES-128 (default), AES-256, DES, CAST, DES-40CP, CAST-40, or NULL (no encryption). The hash algorithms negotiated for both phases are the same – MD5 and SHA1: The default hash algorithm is different for each phase: MD5 for phase II and SHA1 for phase I.

In addition to the algorithms used, mathematical groups are decided upon. In the DH key computation is based on mathematical groups. A group sets the length of the key in terms of bits. The longer the key, the harder it is to break and the more CPU cycles required to generate.

Renegotiating Lifetimes

IKE Phase I is more process intensive than IKE phase II, and therefore performed less frequently. The IKE SA is valid for a specific period of time and must be renegotiated. The IPSec SA is valid for an even shorter period of time requiring the IKE phase II to be performed more frequently.

The period between renegotiations is referred to as the lifetime. The shorter the lifetime, the more secure the IPSec tunnel; it but increases the number of process intensive IKE negotiations. The longer the lifetime, the quicker future VPN connections are be set up. By default, IKE phase I negotiations occurs once a day, while IKE phase II occurs every hour.

Perfect Forward Secrecy

The DH key is computed once and used several times during phase II. The keys used in phase II are mathematically based on the DH key created in phase I. Subsequently, the used of a single DH key can weaken the strength of future keys. If one key is compromised, subsequent keys can be comprised more easily.

Perfect Forward Secrecy (PFS) is a condition where the compromise of a current session key or long-term private key does not cause the compromise of preceding and subsequent keys. PFS mode is offered by VPN-1 Power to meet this requirement. With PFS enabled, a new DH key is generated during phase II and renewed for each key exchange. The DH group used during PFS mode is configurable between groups 1, 2, 5 and 14. Group 2 is the default.

Subnets and Security Associations

By default, a VPN tunnel is created for the complete subnets that hosts reside, not just for the hosts themselves. When communicating between two hosts in different subnets protected by gateways, a total of four SAs are established when a VPN tunnel is created:

- SA between the two gateways
- SA between the subnet and their respective gateway (2)
- SA between the two subnets.

By disabling the option, Support Key Exchange for Subnets, on each gateway, a unique SA can be created for a pair of peers. If the option is disabled on one gateway but not the other, a single host will create a unique SA with a subnet associated with the gateway with the enabled option.

Public Key Infrastructure

PKI solutions based on X.509 provide an infrastructure for establishing trust between entities based on their mutual trust of the Certificate Authority (CA).

IKE standards recommend the use of PKI in VPN environments. A VPN module involved in establishing a VPN tunnel must have an RSA key pair and a certificate issued by a trusted CA. The certificate includes information about the module's identity, its public key, CRL retrieval details and CA signature.

Different Methods of Support

VPN solutions support the following situations:

- Multiple CA Support for Single VPN Tunnel
- Support for non-ICA CAs
- CA Hierarchy.

Trusting External CAs

A prerequisite for establishing VPN tunnels is creating a trusted relationship. This is possible only if the CA signing the peer's certificate is trusted. Trusting a CA involves obtaining and validating the CA's own certificate. After this validation, the details contained in the CA's certificate and its public key can be used to obtain and validate other certificates issued by the same CA.

The ICA will automatically trust all modules managed by the same server that employs it. This is not true for External CAs, so the external CA's certificate must be obtained and trusted.

Subordinate CAs

A subordinate CA is a Certificate Authority that is certified by another Certificate Authority. Subordinate CAs can issue certificates to other subordinate CAs, creating a certification chain or hierarchy.

Enrolling Managed Entities

Enrollment is a process for requesting a CA to issue a certificate for an entity. The process begins with the generation of a key pair. A certificate request is created out of the public key and additional information about the module. The CA type will determine the type of certificate request created and the extent of the enrollment process.

The enrollment process on an internally managed gateway is automatic because the ICA is located on the Server machine. To obtain a certificate from an OPSEC Certified CA, the server takes the details of the module and the public key to encode a PKCS#10 request. The request is delivered manually to the CA by the administrator. The administrator can complete the process by importing the certificate issued by the CA to the server.

Automatic enrollment can be used to obtain a certificate for the gateway. With this, a request for a certificate can be automatically issued for any gateway in the community. The protocols supported by automatic enrollment include SCEP, CMPV1, and CMPV2.

Validating Certificates

When a certificate is received from another entity, the following process is followed to validate the certificate:

1. Verify the certificate signature.
2. Verify the certificate chain has not expired.
3. Verify the certificate chain has not been revoked.

The VPN will also validate the use of the certificate in a given situation, such as confirming the:

- Certificate is authorized to perform the required action
- Correct certificate is used in the negotiation.

Two methods are used to determine the status of a certificate: CRL and Online Certificate Status Protocol (OCSP).

The CRL is available from either an HTTP server or an LDAP server.

If the CRL repository is an HTTP server, the module uses the URL published in the CRL Distributed Point extension located on the certificate and opens an HTTP connection to access the repository. If the CRL is on an LDAP server, VPN will locate the CRL in one of the defined LDAP account units. If the CRL Distribution Point extension exists, the directory entry which the CRL is published or the LDAP URL is published. If the extension does not exist, the attempt to locate the CRL is in the entry of the CA itself in the LDAP server.

OCSP allows applications to identify the state of a certificate and may be used for more timely information on revocations than possible using CRLs, as well as providing other status information. OCSP clients will issue a status request to the OCSP server, acceptance of the certificate is suspended until a response is received from the server. To use OCSP, the root CA must be configured to use this method instead of CRL and will be inherited by subordinate CA's.

WAN Technologies

WAN Properties

Circuit switching allows users to communicate by establishing a channel, or circuit between nodes and terminals. Once a circuit is established, it remains that way until it is released. While the circuit is established, no other user can use it, even when no activity is present. Circuit switches enable non-stop transfers without the requirement for packets and without large amounts of overhead traffic. As a result, the bandwidth available is used at optimal levels.

Packet switching will group all transmitted data into appropriately sized blocks, called packets. Each packet is them transmitted across a shared network independently from all other packets. Where circuit switching will dedicate an entire channel regardless of use, packet switching is intent on utilizing all channels at all time. This, in turn, minimizes the response time and increases the amount of traffic. Packets are buffered and queued requiring additional overhead and resulting in additional delays and throughput.

To manage resources on the network, a physical communication channel is divided into several logical channels or data streams. Each logical stream is comprised of a sequence of packets. The packets are forwarded asynchronously and are held in a buffer until forwarded in a first-in, first out or fair queuing fashion. This process is called dynamic bandwidth allocation or statistical multiplexing.

There are two types of packet switching:

- Connectionless – switching is based on the packet which is labeled with the destination address and sequence number. Each packet sent may take a different route to the destination where the sequence number is used to put all the packets in order to complete the datagram
- Connection oriented – also called virtual circuit switching, where each packet is labeled with a connection ID instead of a destination address. A connection between nodes is set up using the addresses and a virtual circuit is created to allow communication.

Frame Relay

Frame Relay is a connection-oriented, Layer 2 WAN connection technology which operates at speeds from 56 kbps to 45 Mbps.
It is a very flexible solution with several deployment options available. Its main distinction is it operates by statistically multiplexing multiple data streams over a single link.

Data streams are known as virtual circuits (VC) which act like point-to-point circuits, without the physical equipment. Each VC has a committed information rate (CIR) which establishes the minimum bandwidth allowed. Two types of VCs exist: Permanent (PVC) and switched (SVC).

- PVCs are predefined by the provider
- SVCs are created dynamically.

If a Frame Relay network includes PVCs, it is called a full mesh Frame Relay network. Fully meshed networks have any two sites connected by a PVC. A partial mesh network has some pairs without a direct PVC requiring forwarding of packets through other sites.

Each VC is unique and is tagged with an identifier. The identifier is called a Data Link Connection Identifier (DLCI). The DLCI must be unique and agreed upon by two adjacent Frame Relay devices, but they do not have to be the same across the entire frame relay. Valid DLCI numbers are 16 – 1007 (0-15 and 1008-1023 are reserved). The DCLI defines the logical connection between the Frame Relay (FR) switch and the CPE.

FR devices have two roles:

- Data terminal equipment (DTE)
- Data circuit-terminating equipment (DCE).

The DTE/DCE relationship is Layer 2 and normally electric. The DTE/DCE relationship at Layer 1 is independent of Layer 2. DTEs are terminating equipment for a specific network and are normally located at customer sites. DCEs are carrier-owned internetworking devices providing clocking and switching services within the network. They perform all the data transmission within a WAN. DCE devices are packet switches.

T-Carrier and E-Carrier

The T-Carrier refers to a several implementations of digitally multiplexed carrier systems of telecommunications. The basic unit of a T-carrier system is the Digital Signal 0 (DS0), which has a transmission rate of 64 kbps. The European version of the T-Carrier is the E-carrier and is incompatible with the T-Carrier technology. Where T-carrier is used within the United States, Japan, and Korea, all other places use E-carrier. The different between the two standards is the number of channels used, which increases the speed for E-carrier systems over T-carrier.

T-carrier uses pulse-code modulation to share a coder and decoder between locations. This is a digital representation of an analog signal. The magnitude of the signal is sampled at uniform intervals and quantized to a series of binary code.

T1 utilizes 24 channels for transmission. Each channel carries a single byte of data. It uses time-division multiplexing to combine multiple signals and transmit. E1 utilizes 32 channels. T3 systems have 672 channels, while E3 systems have 512 Channels.

Digital Subscriber Line

Digital Subscriber Line (DSL) refers to a several technologies that provide digital data transmission over a local telephone network. DSL allows use over the same line and at the same time as the local telephone service.

DSL utilizes frequencies available but not used by typically analog voice transmissions. It utilizes the existing telephone infrastructure for homes and businesses. Specific variants of DSL provide faster speeds over other DSL solutions; but in all cases, the increase in speed sacrifices the distance that a signal travels.

There are three distinctive technologies of DSL, though there are many more in the entire family:

- Asymmetric DSL (ADSL) – the most common implementation. The volume of data flow in greater in one direction than the other, in most cases increasing the "download" capabilities.
- Symmetric DSL (SDSL) – a rate-adaptive DSL with data rates like T1/E1. Typically allows only data on a line with no analog voice support. The data rates are the same in both directions.

- Very High Bitrate DSL (VDSL) – provides faster data transmissions enabling HDTV and VoIP solutions to be implemented. The same data rates are found in both directions.

Cable Modem

Cable Modems provide bi-directional data communication using radio frequency channels over the cable television (CAT5) infrastructure. Broadband Internet is the typical product of cable modems and found in Australia, Europe, North America, and South America. VoIP has enabled telephone services to be supported by a cable modem.

Technically, a cable modem is a network bridge that allows connection to an Ethernet network. It conforms to IEEE 802.1D. It will bridge Ethernet frames between the LAN and the cable network, while modulating and demodulating the data. The cable modem works within the Physical and Data Link layers of the OSI model. Within the Network Layer is treated as an IP host with its own IP address.

Satellite

Communications satellites utilize microwave radio relay technology to enable TV and radio broadcasts and computer equipment. They are highly useful for mobile communications where the host is constantly moving, and communications in the remotest of areas where even access towers for wireless networks do not reach.

Satellite communications utilize broadband data connections; a high speed data transmission where the bandwidth is shared by more than one signal. This is done through signaling over a wide range of frequencies.

Wireless WAN

A Wireless WAN uses mobile telecommunication cellular network technologies. Some commercial computers have WWAN capabilities if they have a cellular radio built in.

Asynchronous Transfer Mode (ATM)

Asynchronous Transfer Mode is implemented as a network protocol for electronic digital data transmissions. Its intended target in development was to allow transport of real-time video conferencing and audio. ATM is packet-oriented that uses asynchronous time-division multiplexing for transport. Unlike IP or Ethernet networks that use variable sized packets, ATM will encode the data into small fixed-sized cells. Its model is connection-oriented and will establish a virtual circuit.

From a technical perspective, cells are different from packets. When dealing with voice communications, timing and sequencing of the data is important and is in real-time. At the destination of the data transmission, if a digitized data of an analog audio signal is missing packets, the receiving application would have to ignore or invent the missing data creating silence or garbage. When using packets, there is always the possibility of delay from queuing within the network, creating "jitter." ATM will break all packets, data, and voice streams into 480byte chucks with a 5 byte header that are then multiplexed.

Synchronous Optical Networking (SONET)

Synchronous Optical Networking is a standardized multiplexing transport protocol which allows multiple digital bit streams to be transmitted over optical fibers. SONET was originally developed to support circuit switched solutions, but is also useful to support ATM frames because of its protocol neutral and transport features. SONET is used in the United States and Canada, while a similar technology, Synchronous Digital Hierarchy (SDH), is used everywhere else.

The basic unit of transmission in SONET is the synchronous transport signal (STS-1) which operates at 51.84 Mbps. The SDH equivalent is the synchronous transport module (STM-1) which is really STS-3 for SONET with a rate of 155.52 Mbps. A packet frame is handled differently with SONET than Ethernet. Instead of sending the header (overhead) then the payload, SONET will interleave the two during transmission until the entire frame is sent. A frame in STS-1 is 810 octets in size, so 3 octets of overhead is sent, then 87 octets of payload repeatedly until the entire frame is sent. The STS-3 frame is 2430 octets in size and will alternate 9 octets of overhead and 261 octets of payload during transmission.

Greater speeds are possible using time-division multiplexing the basic STS-1 signals. When multiplexing three STS-1 signals, a STS-3 frame is created. Higher speeds are available by successfully aggregating multiples of slower circuits. STS-12 is an aggregation of twelve STS-1 signals, or four STS-3 signals.

Optical Carrier is a set of standardized specifications for transmission speeds over Synchronous Network (SONET) fiber optic networks. The designation OC-x provides a method of determining the data rate of the bitstream of a digital signal. Using fiber optics, a basic digital signal can travel at speeds of 51.84 Mbps. This is the speed at the classification of OC-1. OC-3 is three times faster at 155.53 Mbps, while OC-768 has a transmission speed of 39,813.12 Mbps.

10 Gigabit Ethernet (10GbE) is similar to OC-192/STS-192/STM-64 running at 9.953 Gbps. STS-192 is the most commonly deployed solution.

Multiprotocol Label Switching (MPLS)

Multiprotocol Label Switching (MPLS) is used in high-performance telecommunications networks to aid in directing and carrying data between distant network nodes by creating virtual links. It is a scalable mechanism that is protocol agnostic. It will assign labels to data packets which are used to make decisions on forwarding the packet without having to examine the packet contents. As a result, an end-to-end circuit can be created across any transport medium and using any protocol. MPLS is a connection-oriented packet-switching protocol.

Integrated Services Digital Network (ISDN)

Integrated Services Digital Network provides circuit-switched "dial" options. It is used to provide permanent, always-on WAN connectivity usually as back-up systems, should primary connectivity fail. ISDN is the most popular choice for temporary connectivity. The technology uses digital signals with speeds in increments of 64 kbps.

The Basic Rate Interface (BRI) and Primary Rate Interfaces (PRI) are ISDN interfaces. The difference between BRI and PRI is the number of channels that are offered. ISDN channels are divided into two parts: the bearer (B) channel which carries data and the D channel, used to make signaling requests. BRIs are 2B+D, having two B channels and one D channel.

Each B channel has a maximum throughput of 64 kbps and carries encoded pulse code modulation for digital voice, video, or data. The channel is used for HDLC and PPP protocols and can carry packet-switched data communications. Each D channel is used to dial destination phone numbers. They have a bandwidth of 16 kbps for BRI or 64 kbps for PRI and also carry packet-switch data. Different types of ISDN lines are identified by the number of each type of channel.

ISDN protocols fall into three categories:

- E-series
- I-series
- Q-series.

E-series protocols are used for the international telephone numbering plan and ISDN messaging includes E.163 and E.164. I-series protocols included the I.100 and I.400 series. The I.100 protocols are recommendations to describe and define the principles and terminology of ISDN while the I.400 protocols are a standardization of the User-Network Interface (UNI). Q-series protocols include Q.921 and Q.931. Q.921, the Link Access Protocol – D Channel (LAPD), is the data-link protocol used over ISDN's D channel; while Q.931 enables the ISDN call to establish, then maintenance, and termination of logical network connection.

ISDN has three layers:

- Layer 1 – signal framing
- Layer 2 – framing protocols
- Layer 3 – D channel call setup and teardown.

Layer 1 handles the physical layer, specifically frame formats which differ depending on whether the frame is inbound or outbound. Frames are 48 bits long, with 36 bits representing data. Since multiple user devices can be physically attached to one circuit, collisions can result if two terminals transmit simultaneously, without link detention.

Layer 1 also handles encoding and framing specifications. ISDN BRI uses a single encoding scheme and a single option for framing. ISDN PRI has two options for configuring encoding and framing and is based on a digital T1 circuit in North America. T1 circuits use two different encoding schemes: Alternate Mark Inversion (AMI) and Binary 8 with Zero Substitution (B8ZS). The scheme used should match the telephone company providing the ISDN service. For ISDN PRI services in Europe, Australia, and other countries using E1s, the only choice is High Density Bipolar 3 (HDB3).

Framing determines a device's handling of bits on a channel. PRI framing is based on T1 or E1 specifications. The two T1 framing options define 24 64-kbps DS0 channels and 8-kbps management channel used by the telephone company. These options are Super Frame (SF) and Extended Super Frame (ESF). E1's define 32 64-kbps channels and the two options for E1's are CRC-4 or the original line framing defined for E1s.

Layer 2 builds on the physical addressing of the network and allows multiple logical devices to exist on a single physical device. The source and destination process or logical entity must be identified to handle data transmissions. A Terminal Endpoint Identifier (TEI) is an identifier issued by the ISDN switch. If a specific profile is created for the ISDN implementation, each bearer channel will be assigned a Service Profile Identifiers (SPID) by the provider. The TEI provides the physical identifier while the Service Access Point Identifier (SAPI) provides the logical identifier

SPIDs are a part of BRI implementations and specify the services entitled by the switch and the feature set of the ISDN service. They are manually entered into the router's configuration. SPID typically includes a ten-digit phone number of each B channel followed by four additional digits given by the service provider. SPID requirements are dependent on the software revision and the switch. Only the US requires SPID and only by specific switches.

Layer 3 focuses on D channels and supports the protocols, Link Access Procedure on D channel (LAPD), Signaling System 7 (SS7), and Internal Signaling Utility Protocol (ISUP).

Plain Old Telephone Service (POTS)

Plain Old Telephone Services provides the residential and small business service connection of the telephone network utilized in most parts of the world. POTS provide bidirectional voice capabilities with a limited frequency range of 300 to 3400 Hz. It provides many of the services as customer features. Though it has a low bandwidth, it is one of the most reliable communications systems utilized.

Public Switched Telephone Network (PSTN)

The PSTN is the telephony version of the Internet. It is entirely digital and allows for mobile and fixed telephones.

Basic Wireless Network

Clients

A client is any wireless device that uses the access point to enter the network. The devices can include:

- PCMCIA cards
- Compact flash cards

- Ethernet connectors
- Serial connectors
- USB adapters
- PCA adapters
- ISA adapters.

PCMCIA cards, or PC cards, are used in notebook computers and PDAs. They provide a connection between the client and the network. The main difference in most PC cards is the antenna. Some antennas are flat and small, while others are detachable and connected using a cable. Compact Flash Cards, or CF cards, are similar to PC cards in functionality. They are typically used in PDAs and are the size of a matchbook.

Converters are for any device having Ethernet or legacy 9-pin serial ports. They convert network connections into wireless LAN connections. Ethernet converters are external devices that connect using the category 5 (Cat5) cable. They have the ability to convert a large number of wired nodes to wireless in a matter of minutes. Serial devices are used on older equipment such as terminals, telemetry equipment and serial printers.

USB Adapters are plug-n-play devices and use power delivered through the connection from the computer. Some USB clients utilize modular radio cards while others have a fixed internal card.

PCI and ISA adapters are installed inside desktop or server

equipment. Wireless PCI devices are plug-n-play and may come with an "empty" PCI card which requires the insertion of a separate PCMCIA card to function. Most ISA cards are not plug-n-play and require some configuration through a software utility and the operating system. Typically, the administrator has to change the settings of the adapter to match the settings of the operating system. Drivers for PCI and ISA adapters are usually different and provided for by the manufacturer.

When a PC card is used, it is recommended to use an adapter and card from the same manufacturer. The increased demand of wireless capability has caused most computer manufacturers to include a fixed adapter in new equipment, particularly notebook computers and personal devices.

Wireless adapters are installed using:

- Drivers
- Manufacturer's wireless utilities.

Drivers are typically included with the software. Most adapters are plug-and-play, so a prompt for the software is made when the client device is installed. Some devices, such as Ethernet and Serial converters, do not use any special drivers.

Utilities provided by manufacturers can range in functionality from simple connectivity to a full suite of utilities, including:

- Site Survey Tools

- Spectrum analyzer
- Power and speed monitoring
- Profile configuration
- Link status monitor
- Link testing.

Site survey tools can be used to:

- Find networks
- Identify MAC address or access points
- Quantify signal strength
- Quantify signal-to-noise ratios
- Identify interfering access points.

Spectrum analyzer software will find interfering sources and overlapping wireless LAN channels.

Power and speed configuration utilities monitor the behavior of the wireless link at any given time.

Profile configuration utilities assist in changing from one wireless network to another by creating a profile for each network.

Link status monitor utilities allow users to view a variety of components including:

- Packet errors
- Successful transmissions
- Link viability

- Connection speed
- Configurable parameters.

Though the functionality of the utilities can vary greatly, the configurable parameters are typically the same. They include:

- Infrastructure mode /Ad Hoc mode
- SSID
- Channel
- WEP Keys
- Authentication type.

Using Access Points

When a wireless LAN client is initially installed, configured, and powered, the first action it will take is to scan, or "listen," for any wireless networks within range. Scanning is performed before any other action in order to find the network. Two types of scanning are possible:

- Passive scanning
- Active scanning.

When scanning for a network, the client is in search for an access point. Its search is aided by a series of "clues" left by the access point in the form of service set identifiers (SSID) and beacons.

A SSID is a unique, case sensitive, alphanumeric value or 2-32 characters used as a network name by wireless LANs. The purpose of a network name server is to:

- Segment the network
- Secure the network
- Process joining a network.

The SSID value is sent in beacons, probe requests, probe responses and other types of frames. A wireless client has to be configured for the correct SSID in order to join a network.

Each access point is configured with a SSID, which is sometimes referred to as the ESSID. This is usually performed manually by an administrator, though some stations have the ability to use any SSID value. In order for a client to work and roam seamlessly, the client and access point must be configured with matching SSIDs.

Beacon management frames, or beacons for short, are short frames sent from the access point to stations or station-to-station to organize and synchronize wireless communications. Several functions are fulfilled by beacons, including:

- Time Synchronization
- FH or DS Parameter Sets
- SSID Information
- Traffic Indication Map (TIM)
- Supported Rates.

Clients are synchronized using a timestamp given at the exact time of transmission. When a client receives the beacon, it will change its clock to match the clock of the access point. Time synchronization is essential to ensure that time-sensitive functions, such as frequency hopping, is performed correctly.

Within the beacon is a beacon interval which communicates how often the client can expect beacons. A beacon contains information to support the spread spectrum technology:

- Hop and dwell parameters and hop sequences for FHSS systems
- Channel information for DSSS systems.

Beacons contain the SSID of the network. Stations look to the beacon for that SSID. When found, the station looks at the MAC address where the beacon originated and sends an authentication request to communicate with the access point. If a station can accept any SSID, it will attempt to join the first access point it finds or the access point with the strongest signal.

The TIM acts as an indicator of sleeping stations which have queued packets at the access point. The information is shared to all associated stations by each beacon. Synchronized stations will power up their receivers, listen for the beacon and check the TIM for listings. If the station is not listed, the receiver is powered down and it continues sleeping.

The standard used by the hardware will determine the speeds supported by the wireless network. The supported speeds are communicated to the stations through the beacon.

Passive scanning is the process of listening for beacons on each channel for a specific period of time after initialization. The beacons can be sent by either access points or clients and the scanning station will catalog relevant characteristics of each sending station based on the beacons. This continues until the SSID of the network it wants to join is identified.

In a network with multiple access points, the SSID may be broadcasted by more than one access point. In these cases, the station will attempt to join using the access point with the strongest signal strength and the lowest bit error code (BER). The BER is the ratio of corrupted packets to good packets which is determined by the Signal-to-Noise Ratio of the signal.

Passive scanning continues after the station is associated with an access point. This encourages a viable connection with the network as it saves time reconnecting in the event that the client is disconnected. The reconnection is enabled because the passive scan logged a list of available access points and their characteristics, such as:

- Channel
- Signal strength
- SSID.

With this information, the station can quickly identify the best access point to use. This also aids in roaming stations.

Roaming happens as the station moves from one access point to another typically because the station itself is in motion which is possible for mobile computing. The trigger for finding a new access point is the decrease of the signal strength to a specified low level.

To architect wireless network solutions to support roaming, the specified overlap between access points is 20-30%. This overlap allows seamless disconnection and reconnection without the user's knowledge.

Active scanning will send a probe request frame from a wireless station when they are actively seeking a network to join. The probe request will either contain the SSID of the network they wish to connect to or a broadcast SSID. If the probe request has a specific SSID, only access points supporting that SSID will respond with a probe response frame. If a broadcast SSID is sent, all access points will respond. The purpose of probing in this manner is to locate specific access points from which to attach to a network.

The information provided by the probe response frames is almost identical to the information found in beacons. The difference is the exclusion of the timestamp and the TIM. The signal strength of the probe response frame will assist in determining the access point the station will attempt to associate. The chosen access point is typically based a strong signal strength and low BER.

Connecting to a wireless LAN consists of two separate sub-processes:

- Authentication

- Association.

Authentication is on the acceptance of the radio PC card, not the user. Association refers to connectivity at Layer 2. Connecting to a wireless LAN starts with authentication, a process where a wireless nose, such as a PC card, USB Client, or adapter, has its identify verified by the network.

Sometimes the authentication process is null which allows a client and access point to associate without any special identity required. This is often the case when new access points or clients are installed in default configurations.

Authentication starts when the client sends an authentication request frame to the access point. The access point will accept or deny the request and notify the client of the decision through an authentication response frame. Sometimes this decision is made by the access point, or it may be configured to pass the request along to an upstream authentication server, such as RADIUS.

Once a wireless client has been authenticated, the association process starts. To be associated means the client is allowed to pass data through an access point. This ensures that the client communicates with the network through the access point.

When a client wants to connect, the authentication request is sent and an authentication response is received. At this point, an association request frame is sent to the access point. An association response frame is sent back confirming the association or not.

The complete process of authentication and association has three distinct states:

- Unauthenticated and unassociated
- Authenticated and unassociated
- Authenticated and associated.

When a wireless node is completely disconnected from the network and unable to pass frames through an access point, the client is considered to be in a state of being unauthenticated and unassociated. Different vendors refer to this state differently in their access points' association table, which tracks whether a client has completed the authentication process or attempted and failed. The typically notation in the table is “unauthentication.”

When the wireless client has passed the authentication process but has still not associated with the access point, they are in the state of authenticated and unassociated. The association table typically notes this state as “authenticated.” The processes of authentication and association happen very quickly, in milliseconds.

When the wireless client is completely connected to the network and sending and receiving data through the access point, it is considered to be in the state of being authenticated and associated and its notation in the association table is “associated.”

Given these three states, it is best that most advance security steps are performed when the client is attempting to authenticate.

Wireless Authentication

Two methods of authentication are specified by IEEE 802.11 standards:

- Open System authentication
- Shared Key authentication.

Open System authentication is the simplest and most secure of the two methods. The IEEE 802.11 specifies this as the default setting for wireless LAN equipment.

The method is one of null authentication. Authentication is given based on the possession of the right SSID. The process is effective in both secure and non-secure environments.

The process of Open System Authentication is:

- A request is made by the client to associate with the access point
- The access point authenticates the client and sends a positive response.

Though there are several reasons for using Open System authentication, the two primary reasons are:

- It is the most secure of the two methods
- It requires no configuration at all since it is the default setting for all 802.11 devices.

A wireless LAN administrator has the option of using WEP encryption with Open System authentication. If this option is taken, no verification of the WEP key happens until the client is authenticated and associated.

The use of WEP is required for Shared Key authentication. The WEP key is typically manually entered by the administrator on both the client and the access point.

The process of Shared Key Authentication follows:

- A request is made to associate with an access point by the client
- The access points issues a challenge to the client, which is a randomly generated plain text
- The client responds to the challenge by encrypting the change text with the WEP key set on the client and sending it back
- The access point decrypts the response to ensure the encryption matches the WEP key
- If the WEP keys match, authentication completes by sending the client a positive response. If a match is not made, a negative response is not made.

Shared Key authentication is not considered secure because the access point transmits the challenge text in the clear and receives the same challenge text encrypted. This allows a hacker using a sniffer to see both the plaintext challenge and the encrypted challenge and create a simple cracking program to derive the WEP key.

The WEP key is commonly confused with "shared secret." a shared secret is a string of numbers or text that provides an alternative test to authenticate. Authentication documents, or certificates, are another form of authentication. Both methods have traditionally been manually configured, but applications have started to automatically work.

Wireless Communication Standards

IEEE 802.11 standards

When it comes to information technology in the United States, the IEEE is the primary standards maker for most subjects. They utilize the laws created by the FCC as guidelines to create standards.

IEEE 802.11 is the recognized technology standard for wireless LANs. The standard consists of a main body and several amendments. The most referenced parts of the standard include:

- 802.11
- 802.11a
- 802.11b
- 802.11g
- 802.11n

The 802.11 is the main body of the standard describing the operation of wireless LANs. The standard contains the transmission technology descriptions for Direct Sequence Spread Spectrum (DSSS), Frequency Hopping Spread Spectrum (FHSS), and infrared.

The 802.11 standard describes the operation of DSSS system at 1 Mbps and 2 Mbps data rate transfer. Systems that can operate at other data rates including 1 Mbps and 2 Mbps, the device is 802.11-compliant. However, the system must be operating at 1 or 2 Mbps (802.11 compliant mode) to be expected to communicate with other 802.11 compliant devices.

IEEE provides one of two standards for the operations of FHSS systems. The IEEE standard describes FHSS system sat 1 and 2 Mbps. The same compatibility issues are in place as with DSSS systems.

802.11 focuses on products that operate within the 2.4 GHz ISM band. The exception is infrared, a light-based technology which is covered by the standard but does not fall in the 2.4 GHz ISM band.

802.11b is often referred to as “high-rate” and Wi-Fi. The original standard provided a basic description for operating wireless LANs based on the technology at the time of adoption. Technology grew and eventually outgrew the standard. 802.11b was a successful attempt to update the standard.

It's considered high-rate because it describes the operation of DSSS systems at 1, 2, 5.5 and 11 Mbps. By default, 802.11b-compliant devices are 802.11-compliant. This allows backward compatibility and allows upgrades to existing networks without replacing core hardware, providing a low-cost solution to remain competitive.

The high data rate provided by 802.11b-compliant devices is possible by the use of a different coding technique. The system is still a direct sequencing system, but the chip is coded using CCK rather than Barker Code. The information is modulated different as well allowing a greater amount of data to be transferred in the same time frame. 802.11b products will only operate in the 2.4 GHz ISM band between 2.4000 and 2.4835 GHz.

The 802.11a describes wireless operations in the 5 GHz UNII bands. Operating in the UNII bands make 802.11a devices incompatible with all other devices compliant to other 802.11 series of standards, because 5 GHz frequencies do not communicate with systems using 2.4 GHz frequencies.

With the UNII bands, devices can achieve data rates of 6, 9, 12, 18, 24, 36, 48, and 54 Mbps. Proprietary technology can raise the data rate as high as 108 Mbps using rate doubling. However, 802.11a specifies data rates of only 6, 12, and 24 Mbps. To be 802.11a-compliant, devices must support these data rates at the very least. The maximum data rate specified by the standard is 54 Mbps.

802.11g standard provides data speeds similar to 802.11a but is backwards compatible to 802.11 devices. The standard still operates in the 2.4 GHz ISM band, but utilizes Orthogonal Frequency Division Multiplexing (OFDM) modulation which allows higher data rates. Backwards compatibility allows QSPK modulation to communicate with slower 802.11 and 802.11b compliant devices.

The primary difference with 802.11n is the inclusion of option modes and configurations. This allows manufacturers to maintain baseline performance parameters while accommodating different customer demands. The options are not required to be supported to be 802.11n compliant. OFDM modulation has been improved to allow an attainable raw data rate of 65 Mbps, up from 54 Mbps in other standards.

One of the biggest changes is the adoption of Multiple Input Multiple Output (MIMO), which exploits multipathing by splitting the data stream into multiple parts, called spatial streams, and transmitting each stream from different antennas. 4 spatial streams are supported by the standard. Using 2 spatial streams instead of one essentially doubles the data rate, though power consumption and cost also increases. The technique used to split the data stream is called space-division multiplexing.

802.11n is backwards compatible with 802.11b and 802.11g
Below is a comparison of the different standards:

	802.11a	**802.11b**	**802.11g**	**802.11n**
Frequency	5 GHz	2.4 GHz	2.4 GHz	2.4 GHz and 5 GHz
Throughput	27 Mbps	5 Mbps	22 Mbps	144 Mbps
Net Bit Rate	54 Mbps	11 Mbps	54 Mbps	600 Mbps
Gross Bit Rate	72 Mbps		128 Mbps	

Maximum Indoor Range	50 feet	150 feet	150 feet	300 feet
Maximum Outdoor Range	100 feet	300 feet	300 feet	600 feet
Channel Width	20 MHz	20 MHz	20 MHz	20 or 40 MHz
Spatial Streams	1	1	1	1, 2, 3, or 4
Modulation	OFDM	DSSS CCK	DSSS CCK OFDM	DSSS CCK OFDM

Authentication and Encryption

Wired Equivalent Privacy (WEP) is an algorithm used to secure IEEE 802.11 wireless networks. Since radio frequencies are used to transmit messages over wireless networks, eavesdropping is a major concern. The intention of WEP is to provide confidentiality at a level experienced with wired networks. The algorithm provides this by utilizing a stream cipher RC4 to make messages confidential and, for integrity, using a SRC-32 checksum.

The standard 64-bit WEP utilizes a 40-bit key and a 34-bit initialization vector (IV) to create the traffic key. The 128bit WEP is composed of a 104-bit key and 24-bit IV. The larger 256-bit WEP key is 232-bits key and 24-bits IV. The keys are created using hexadecimal characters: 26 for the 128-bit key and 58 for the 256-bit key. Each character represents 4 bits. The larger the key, the harder it is to crack.

WEP has two methods of authentication:

- Open System Authentication
- Shared Key Authentication.

Using Open System Authentication, the wireless client will connect to an access point without providing credentials. The client will authenticate itself and associate itself to the access point. WEP is used to encrypt the data frames.

In Shared Key Authentication, the wireless client does provide credentials as WEP does perform authentication. Once authentication has been successful, the client is associated with the access point and WEP will encrypt the data frames. To authentication, WEP utilizes a four-phase handshake:

- The client sends an authentication request to the access point
- The access point sends the client a clear-text message as a challenge
- The client encrypts the challenge text using the configured WEP key and sends the encrypted text in another authentication request
- The access point decrypts the challenge and compares with the original clear-text message. If a match exists, the access point will associate itself with the client.

Temporal Key Integrity Protocol (TKIP) is a security protocol for wireless networking. It was designed to be a replacement for WEP without requiring the replacement of any hardware. TKIP introduces three security features to overcome WEP flaws:

- A key mixing function combines the secret root key with the initialization vector before performing the RC4 initialization
- A sequence counter was implemented to protect from replay attacks allowing out-of-order packets to be rejected
- The implementation of a 64-bit message integrity check which was called MICHAEL.

TKIP was created in a joint venture between the IEEE 802.11i task group and the Wi-Fi Alliance. The Wi-Fi Alliance chose to endorse TKIP under the name Wi-Fi Protected Access (WPA) in 2002. When IEEE officially endorsed TKIP in 2004, the Wi-Fi Alliance adopted the full specification under the name WPA2. In efforts to make WPA more secure, the development and inclusion of Extensible Authentication Protocol (EAP) has been performed.

EAP is a layer 2 protocol that allows plug-ins at either end of a link to utilize several methods of authentication. It is a flexible replacement for PAP and CHAP under PPP which are used for user authentication on wired LANs and support using passwords. EAP provides the same functionality on wireless LANs.

In the 802.1x standard model, network authentication consists of three pieces, the supplicant (client), the authenticator (access point), and the authentication server.

The process for 802.11x and EAP follows:

1. The client makes a request to associate with an access point.
2. The access point requests the EAP identity of the client.
3. The client responds to the access point's request who forwards the response to the Authentication Server.
4. The Authentication Server makes a request for EAP authentication to the access point who forwards to the client.
5. The client responds to the request back to the access point who forwards to the Authentication Server.
6. The Authentication Server verifies the association to the access point and further to the client.

There are several types of EAP authentication that are used to secure a wireless LAN connection. Understanding the EAP types will assist in understanding the authentication methods used like:

- Passwords
- Key generation
- Mutual authentication
- Protocol.

Some of the commonly deployed EAP authentication types include:

- EAP-MD-5 Challenge – the earliest EAP authentication type duplicating the CHAP password protection on wireless networks
- EAP-Cisco Wireless – also called Lightweight Extensible Authentication Protocol (LEAP), this type is primarily used in Cisco wireless LAN access points to provide security

during credential exchange, encrypt data transmission using dynamically generated WEP keys, and support mutual authentication

- EAP-TLS (Transport Layer Security) – provides certification-based, mutual authentication of the client and the network
- EAP-TTLS – an extension of EAP-TLS requiring only server side certificates and can support legacy password protocols
- EAP-SRP (Secure Remote Password) – a secure, password-based authentication and key exchange protocol used to securely authenticate clients to servers where the user must memorize a small secret, such as a password without any other information available
- EAP-SIM (GSM) – used as a mechanism for Mobile IP network access authentication and registration key generation using the GSM Subscriber Identity Module (SIM).

User authentication is usually accomplished using a Remote Authentication Dial-In User Service (RADIUS) server and some type of database such as:

- Native RADIUS
- NDS
- Active Directory
- LDAP.

When a user or device attempts to gain access to a network resource, they send a request to the Network Access Server (NAS) with the appropriate access credentials using a link-layer protocol. The NAS will send a RADIUS Access Request message to the RADIUS server using the RADIUS protocol, which works on the application layer. The request to RADIUS includes the access credentials, such as name and password or security certificate. The RADIUS server confirms that the information contained in the request is correct using an authentication scheme like PAP, CHAP, or EAP. The RADIUS server will perform that confirmation by checking a locally stored database or other external source of information.

The server will return one of three responses to the NAS:

- Access Reject – The user is unconditionally denied access to all network resources
- Access Challenge – Additional information from the user is requested
- Access Accept – The user is granted access.

Once network access has been granted, the NAS will start the accounting process by sending a message to the RADIUS server to indicate the network access has been initiated by the user. This message, indicating the start of the network session, contains information about the user's identity, the network address, the point of attachment, and the unique session identifier. It also has a “start” value attributed to Acct-Status-Type. The status of the session is updated periodically using an accounting packet with the Acct-Status-Type attribute of “interim-update.” The interim record contains information on the current session duration and the data usage. When the network access is closed, a final accounting packet with the attribute of “stop” is sent from the NAS to the RADIUS server. This accounting process is used for general network monitoring, statistical reporting, and billing of network usage.

Wireless LAN Attacks

Four general types of attacks are often used against wireless LANs:

- Passive attacks
- Active attacks
- Jamming attacks
- Man-in-the-middle attacks.

Passive Attacks

Passive attacks involve eavesdropping: a simple yet effective attack on wireless LANs. Essentially, the effort utilizes sniffers or customer application to gather information about the wireless network from a distance.

Active Attacks

The purpose of an active attack is to perform a function on the network, including:

- Obtaining data on the network
- Using the access for malicious purposes
- Changing configurations.

Jamming

The purpose of jamming is to shut down the wireless network. Jamming is done by overloading the RF signal, typically by using a high-powered RF signal generator or sweep generator.

Jamming can be intentional or non-intentional.

To resolve a jamming attack, the source of the jamming must be identified. Spectrum analyzers can be used for this purpose

Man-in-the-Middle Attacks

A man-in-the-middle attack is comprised of two access points and used to hijack mobile clients. On an established and legitimate network, mobile clients are connected to the access point. In a MITM attack, a malicious hacker uses another access point with a stronger signal than the original access point. The wireless clients now associate to this stronger rogue access point.

Some event must trigger the clients switch to the rogue access point. Some clients may do so accidentally as part of any roaming done by the system. An all-band interference event can force roaming to happen to all clients in the area.

Of course, the hacker must know and configure the rogue access point with the SSID used by the network.

Securing Wireless LANs

A few things to look at when securing wireless LANs:

- Manually configure WPA setting
- Restrict availability of WLAN clients
- Use WEP and WPA compliant hardware
- Manually configure WLAN settings for WPA.

Security solutions are emerging, including:

- Key management
- Wireless VPNs
- Key Hopping Technologies
- Temporal Key Integrity Protocol (TKIP)
- AES Based Solutions
- Wireless Gateways
- 802.1x and EAP.

Business Continuity Planning

Business Continuity Planning is consists of planning and implementation of maintaining critical business operations in the event of a major failure or disaster. Disaster Recovery Planning is those efforts to provide an effective approach to recovering all business operations after the occurrence of such an event.

Network Evaluation

Successful planning begins with understanding the current capabilities of the organization.

When assessing the current capabilities of the network in relation to supporting business and technical requirements, four areas should be evaluated:

- Physical – topology, devices, connectivity, speed, media types
- Logical – protocols, address assignments, existing access lists
- Traffic – network, local and external traffic
- Management – management tools , stations, monitoring tools, analyzers and probes.

Specific activities include:

- Physical Assessment
    - Identify LAN technologies used

    - Document WAN circuits
    - Identify WAN technologies used
- Logical Assessment
    - Determine routed protocols
    - Identify the IP address assignment scheme
    - Identify the Novell IPX address assignments
    - Identify AppleTalk address assignments
    - Determine any addressing or broadcast filtering
    - Document the Layer 3 architecture
- Traffic Assessment
    - Document the traffic flows
    - Determine segment traffic patterns
    - Locate servers
    - Determine internal and external traffic
- Management Assessment
    - Determine tools set used for managing network
    - Determine management stations
    - Identify capacity or performance monitoring tools
    - Identify any available network protocol analyzer
    - Identify any RMON probes in use.

Corporate profile information will provide an understanding of the type of business conducted by the company and the business constraints present. Significant to designing the network is understanding:

- Business goals and business type
- Corporate structure
- Geographical structure

- Staffing (current and future)
- Policies and politics.

Continuity Planning

The preservation of business operations in the face of major disruptions is a primary focus of business continuity planning (BCP) and disaster recovery planning (DRP). The activities include the preparation, processes, and practices to protect the critical business processes from the impact of disruption and recovery of business operations.

The purpose of continuity planning is driven by the existence of:

- Terrorist attack
- Natural disaster
- Internal and external audit oversight
- Legislative and regulatory requirements.

Industry and professional standards are in place which provide guidelines for effective business continuity including:

- National Standard on Preparedness, or NFPA 1600
- ISO 17799
- Defense Security Service (DSS)
- National Institute of Standards and Technology (NIST)
- Standard of Due Care.

BCP/DRP processes focus on increasing the probability of surviving a major disruption by concentrating on potential loss categories, which include

- Revenue loss
- Extra expenses
- Compromised customer service
- Embarrassment or loss of confidence.

Continuity Planning Process

The major phases for business continuity planning include:

- Project Initiation
- Current State Assessment
- Design and Development
- Implementation
- Management.

Project Initiation Phase

The project initiation phase involves all the pre-planning activities required to start BCP/DRP efforts properly. The primary goal is to adequately identify management intentions and commitment.

The activities common for this phase are:

- Establishing the scope and objectives for continuity planning
- Gaining management support
- Building a project team for continuity planning activities

and defining the roles within the team

- Defining project resource requirements
- Identifying and leveraging existing and planned disaster avoidance preparations.

The development of the scope should focus on:

- Disaster recovery planning (DRP)
- Business continuity planning (BCP)
- Crisis management planning (CMP)
- Continuous availability (CA)
- Incident command systems (ICS).

Management support is required to:

- Formalize a continuity planning policy
- Establish and manage a budget
- Define continuity planning metrics.

Current State Assessment Phase

The current state assessment phase consists of activities to provide appropriate information about the current environment to make informed decisions about future business planning needs.

The activities will complete:

- A threat analysis
- A business impact assessment (BIA)
- An assessment of the current state of the continuity

planning process
- A benchmark or peer review.

The result of this phase will provide a comprehensive understanding of the strategies, goals and objectives of the organization.

The assessment should cover various areas including:

- Enterprise business processes analysis
- People and organizations
- Time dependencies
- Motivation, risks and control objectives
- Budgets
- Technical issues and constraints.

Specific security concerns involve:

- Physical security
- Personnel security
- Environmental security
- Information security.

Design and Development Phase

Using the information gathered in the current state assessment phase, the project team creates the most effective and efficient recovery strategies. The primary activities for this stage include:

- Developing and designing appropriate strategies
- Developing the crisis management plan (CMP) and

structures for BCP and DRP

- Developing the required infrastructure testing and maintenance activities
- Planning the acquisition of recovery resources
- Designing the initial acceptance testing of the plans.

One of the key considerations in disaster recovery is predetermining the need for alternative recovery sites:

- Cold sites – IT locations with the capability but not the equipment
- Warm sites – IT locations with the capability and some equipment
- Hot sites – IT locations with the capability and equipment
- Mobile sites – remote mobile IT locations for temporary use
- Multiple processing sites – provides workload balancing when one location fails
- Workspace and facilities – provided by commercial recovery site vendors
- Virtual business partners – utilizes outside business partner's IT when required.

Implementation Phase

The project team works with the organization's business process owners to implement:

- Continuity plans
- Short-term and long-term testing

- Short-term and long-term maintenance strategies
- Training, awareness, and education processes
- Management processes.

Management Phase

Manages the day-to-day activities of continuity planning.

Legislation Related to Business Continuity

Requirements for business continuity are sometimes guided by the need to comply with legislation. Some related legislations include:

- Health Insurance Portability and Accountability Act (HIPAA) of 1996
- Gramm-Leach-Bliley (BLB) Act of 1999
- Uniting and Strengthening America by Providing Appropriate Tools Required to Intercept and Obstruct Terrorism Act of 2001 or Patriot Act.

Law, Investigations and Ethics

Legal Concepts

Within the United States, laws may be the result of:

- Statutory law which becomes United States Code after being enacted by Congress
- Administrative law is part of the Code of Federal Regulations which is enacted by agencies of the executive branch
- Case law exists within the judicial branch and documents the legal precedents of the court.

Categories of Law

Major legal systems are categorized as:

- Common or criminal law
- Civil or code law
- Customary law
- Religious
- Mixed law.

Common law is based on principles developed over generations and recognized by courts, but not codified in any legislative fashion.

Criminal law is based on common law, statutory law, or a combination of both which typically results in punishment by imprisonment and fines for crimes against society.

Civil laws address crimes against an individual or organization and results in financial damages.

Administration, or regulatory, law provides sanctions for violations.

Evidence

Evidence is important for supporting conclusions related to events. Depending on how the evidence is used, there are two types of evidence that an organization would be concerned with:

- Evidence for audit purposes, including
  - Physical examination
  - Documentation
  - Observation
  - Injury
  - Mechanical accuracy
  - Analytical procedures
  - Confirmation
- Evidence of legal procedures, including
  - Best evidence
  - Secondary
  - Direct
  - Conclusive
  - Circumstantial
  - Corroborative
  - Opinion

- Hearsay.

For evidence to be admissible in a court of law, it must meet three standards:

- Relevancy – must provide information related to the crime
- Reliability – cannot be tampered with, requiring a documented chain of custody
- Legality – must be gathered within the parameters of the law and respecting the rights of the accused.

For any event requiring an investigation, a computer incident response team (CIRT) is the best choice to lead the effort.

The planned outcome of the investigation should be an early decision, to determine the appropriate scope and actions of the investigating team. If criminal prosecution is the goal, digital forensic procedures must be followed and appropriate law enforcement agency involved.

Intellectual Property Laws

Some information found in an organization may be considered intellectual property and protected by one or more legal mechanisms:

- Copyrights – protects original works of authorship which last for 70 years after the death of the author
- Patents – protects novel inventions for 17 years from the time of invention
- Trademarks – protects words, symbols, or other marking that distinguish the source of a product or service

- Trade secrets – confidential business secrets not released to outsiders which are protected if reasonable precautions are taken to ensure protect those secrets.

Ethics

Ethics in computing deals with the proper use of computers. Specific topics include:

- How computers impact the workplace
- Computer crime and security
- Privacy and anonymity
- Intellectual property rights related to software ownership
- Professional responsibility and globalization of networking.

Fallacies in Computer Ethics

- Computer Game Fallacy – computers can prevent cheating or wrong doing.
- Law-Abiding Citizen Fallacy – laws are in place to guide proper computer use
- Shatterproof Fallacy – little harm can come from simply using a computer as intended
- Candy-from-a-Baby Fallacy – if it can be done easily using a computer, it must be appropriate to do
- Hacker's Fallacy – hacking is appropriate if used as a tool to learn
- Free Information Fallacy – information should be free.

Hacker ethics incorporates:

- Access to computers should be limited and total
- Information should be free
- Authority is mistrusted
- Skills in hacker should be the only criteria of judgment
- Computers provide beauty and art
- Computers improve life.

Ethic Codes and Organizations

The various codes and organizations that provide guidelines for ethics include:

- The Code of Fair Information Practices
- Internet Architecture Board and RFC 1087
- Computer Ethics Institute (CEI)
- National Conference on Computing and Values
- The Working Group on Computer Ethics
- National Computer Ethics and Responsibilities Campaign
- $(ISC)^2$ Code of Ethics.

Legal considerations are a pertinent subject of security implementation, covering:

- Legal protection from attack
- Compliance to legal standards
- Legality of current and future operations.

(ISC)2 Code of Ethics

The Code of Ethics has two preamble elements:

- "Safety of the commonwealth, duty to our principals, and to each other requires that we adhere, and be seen to adhere, to the highest ethical standards of behavior
- Therefore, strict adherence to this Code is a condition of certification".

Four required canons of ethics exist:

- Protect society, the commonwealth, and the infrastructure
- Act honorably, honestly, justly, responsibly, and legally
- Provide diligent and competent service
- Advance and protect the profession.

RFC 1087

The Internet Activities Board Code of Ethics is defined in RFC 1087. Any activity is considered unethical and unacceptable if it purposefully:

- Seeks to gain unauthorized access to Internet-based resources
- Disrupts the intended use of the Internet
- Wastes resources through these actions
- Destroys the integrity of computer-based information
- Compromises the privacy of user.

Practice Exam

Question 1

Access control focuses on providing what abilities?

A. Confidentiality, Integrity, and Availability
B. Identification, Authentication, Authorization, and Monitoring
C. Identification, Authentication, and Association
D. Separation of Duties, Least Privilege, and Classification

Question 2

What is the advantage of smart cards over memory cards?

A. Information can be divided into sections
B. Smart cards are smaller in size
C. Information can be sent through a smart card
D. The data stored on the card can be protected

Question 3

Which of the following modes of the Data Encryption Standard operate like a stream mode cipher? (Choose all that apply)

A. Output Feedback Mode
B. Cipher Feedback Mode
C. Electronic Codebook Mode
D. Cipher Clock Chaining Mode

Question 4

Which allocation process of the Dynamic Host Configuration Protocol ensures that an individual client will retain the same IP address each time they log onto the network?

A. Dynamic
B. Static
C. Automatic
D. Customized

Question 5

Which of the following operations is not conducted by the Advanced Encryption Standard on a message?

A. Shift rows
B. Transpose bytes
C. Mix columns
D. Add roundkey

Question 6

Access Points can be configured to perform different functions based on the needs of the business. What mode of configuration allows a wireless access point to connect to a wired network?

A. Bridge
B. Repeater
C. Basic
D. Root

Question 7

Which port category does port 1040 fall into?

A. Well-known port
B. Dynamic port
C. Designated port
D. Private port

Question 8

Intrusion Detection Systems can be used to identify what type of scanning on the network?

A. Active Port Scanning
B. Vulnerability scanning
C. Network Scanning
D. Passive Port Scanning

Question 9

What type of security controls ensures compliance to the security policy?

A. Preventative
B. Deterrent
C. Directive
D. Compensating

Question 10

Which security model handles both confidentiality and integrity concerns that may be present for an organization?

A. Access Matrix Model
B. Biba Model
C. Clark-Wilson Model
D. Bell-LaPadua Model

Question 11

Which of the following responses to the Network Access Server prevents unconditional access to all network resources?

A. Access Deny
B. Access Reject
C. Access Accept
D. Access Challenge

Question 12

Which of the following port components are not necessary for 802.1x implementation?

A. Client Software
B. Authentication Server
C. Supplicant
D. Authenticator

Question 13

What countermeasures are often adopted to attract potential attackers from high value targets on the network by pretending to be of equal or greater value?

A. Darknets
B. Spoofing
C. Honeypots
D. Man-in-the-Middle

Question 14

Which of the following items is not a phase of DHCP used to acquire an IP address?

A. IP Discovery
B. IP Request
C. IP Acceptance
D. IP Lease Offer

Question 15

When routing information on specific hosts is manually entered into the routing tables of the router, what form of routing is being performed?

A. Link State Routing
B. Dynamic Routing
C. Distance Vector Routing
D. Static Routing

Question 16

Hubs are used to repeat signals through multiple ports and consist of several types. You are supporting a small company of approximately ten employees within a single suite in an office building. They want to connect all their computers together for communications and file sharing only. What is the most appropriate form of hub to use?

A. An intelligent hub performs error detection
B. A passive hub ensures data transmission across the entire network and ideal for small offices
C. A passive hub is the cheapest alternative for a small company
D. An active hub allows signals to be regenerated to allow transport over longer distances

Question 17

Which of the following is an application of Transmission Control Protocol?

A. VoIP
B. Online Gaming
C. Email
D. DNS

Question 18

What type of ciphers are typically found in hardware implementations of cryptography?

A. Block
B. Substitution
C. Stream
D. Transposition

Question 19

Which of the following situations embodies the proper elements to securely identify a user accessing the network to provide the greatest security options?

A. Upon being hired, an employee is provided a guest account which upon first login requires the user to create a new permanent network account and profile which will be used to access basic services and provide information for access to additional resources upon request
B. Upon being hired, a primary network access account is created for the employee to allow access to basic services, including email and network login. A temporary password is provided that must be changed upon first login. Additional access to services and applications must be requested individually and for critical functions additional IDs and passwords may be provided
C. Upon being hired, an account is created for the employee on the spot with a temporary password. At first sign in, the

password must be changed by the user. The user must request access to applications and services required for their job, which are associated to their main account

D. Upon being hired, a network access account is created for the employee to allow access to basic services, including email and network login. Additional access to services and applications must be requested individually and for critical functions additional IDs and passwords may be provided

Question 20

What form of access control do Intrusion Detection Systems fall under?

A. Preventative
B. Compensation
C. Deterrent
D. Detective

Question 21

Which of the following is an example of a Single Sign-On implementation of an authentication system?

A. TACACS+
B. VPN/VLAN
C. SESAME
D. RADIUS

Question 22

Which of the following is not considered a control to maintain message integrity?

A. Checksums
B. Asymmetric Algorithms
C. Message Authentication Code
D. Hash functions

Question 23

Which transport protocol defines a format for packets delivering audio and video data over the Internet?

A. SIP
B. HTTP
C. ICMP
D. RTP

Question 24

Which cryptoanalysis attack performs calculations on the product of two prime numbers to break down the encryption algorithm?

A. Random number generation
B. Factoring attack
C. Replay attack
D. Frequency analysis

Question 25

What is the primary purpose of a firewall?

A. To filter packets based on a set of predefined rules.
B. To provide a barrier from intense areas of heat.
C. To segment internal and external networks.
D. To prevent unauthorized access.

Question 26

Which system form is typically connected to a firewall to allow predefined processes to flow through while blocking all other processes?

A. HIPS
B. HIDS
C. NIPS
D. NIDS

Question 27

Which of the following is an example of CIDR Notation?

A. 192.201.154.32
B. 192.201.154.32/22
C. 11000000.11001001.10011010.00100000
D. 1111:1111:1111:1111:1111:1111:192.201.154.32

Question 28

Which type of attack is described as a process utilizing weaknesses with Internet protocols to establish trust to access systems?

A. Tapping
B. Social Engineering
C. Mobile code
D. Spoofing

Question 29

Which of the following process steps is not part of an Operations Security (OPSEC) implementation?

A. Assessment of Competition
B. Analysis of Threats
C. Assessment of Risk
D. Analysis of Vulnerabilities

Question 30

IPSec is a suite of protocols that provide security support for what IT technology?

A. Peer-to-Peer
B. VLANs
C. VPNs
D. STP

Question 31

Which of the following activities describes when a client moves from one access point to another on a wireless network?

A. Scanning
B. Multicasting
C. Transferring
D. Roaming

Question 32

Which of the following is not a state of a port using the Spanning-Tree Protocol?

A. Blocking
B. Forwarding
C. Talking
D. Listening

Question 33

Which of the following access control models uses graphs to show security permissions between object?

A. Bell-Padua Model
B. Take-Grant Model
C. Access Matrix Model
D. State Machine Model

Question 34

Single loss expectancy is a product of what two variables?

A. Asset value and number of expected failures
B. Exposure factor and availability loss
C. Asset value and exposure factor
D. Asset value and business priority

Question 35

What addressing technique is used to allow private IP addresses to be used and still connect to the Internet?

A. Network Access Translation
B. Supernetting
C. Port Access Translation
D. Subnetting

Question 36

Which of the following technologies can be used optimize network performance by delaying packets entering the network?

A. Traffic Shaper
B. Proxy Server
C. Load Balancer
D. IDS

Question 37

Which layer of the OSI model do hardware devices that connect different network segments without any filtering operate on?

A. Transport Layer
B. Physical Layer
C. Data Link Layer
D. Network Layer

Question 38

End-to-end delivery of data is ensured by what layer of the OSI Model?

A. Physical
B. Network
C. Data Link
D. Transport

Question 39

What is the purpose of defense in depth security solutions?

A. To prevent entry from an attack
B. To mitigate the impact from an attack
C. To confuse potential attackers.
D. To delay entry from an attack.

Question 40

Your company wants to review and improve their current IT capabilities from an ITIL perspective. Which of the following processes should be reviewed or be impacted to improvements in this area? (Choose all that apply)

A. Change Management
B. Incident Management
C. Capacity Management
D. Business Continuity and Disaster Recovery
E. Performance Management

Answer Guide

Question 1

Answer: B

Reasoning: All of the answers are associated with access control. Confidentiality, Integrity, and Availability provide the oversight and goals for all security, including access control solutions, but they are not abilities. Separation of Duties, Least Privilege, and Information Classification are principles for defining access control rules. Association is a processed used in remote access and wireless communication to link two points and though it can be viewed as an ability, it only applies to a small subset of access control. Identification, Authentication, Authorization, and Monitoring encompass all of the functions and features of access control that must be in place in every solution to be effective.

Question 2

Answer: D

Reasoning: Smart cards are generally the same size as memory cards used for identification purposes. Smart cards have numerous benefits but the primary advantage they have over memory cards is that they can protect the data stored on the card, usually through encryption.

Question 3

Answer: A, B

Reasoning: Five modes are available to DES: ECB, CBC, CFB, OFB, and CTR. ECB are the most basic form of DES. All modes of DES are block mode ciphers, however, CFB, OFB, and CTR are designed to act like stream mode ciphers.

Question 4

Answer: C

Reasoning: Automatic allocation sets permanent IP addresses for each client logging into the network. Dynamic allocation will associate any IP address with any person logging into the network temporarily. Static allocation will provide IP addresses to only those clients with a MAC address manually listed in a table on the DHCP server.

Question 5

Answer: B

Reasoning: In AES, bytes are not transposed, they are substituted. When a plaintext message is encrypted using AES, the message is placed into a 128-bit state array with the key in a similar table. Using the key as a guide, the four major operations are performed on the message: substituting bytes, shifting rows, mixing columns, adding roundkeys.

Question 6

Answer: D

Reasoning: The root mode is a default connection and allows wireless access points to connect to the wired network backbone using a wired interface.

Question 7

Answer: C

Reasoning: Ports 0 – 1023 are considered well-known ports; 1024 – 59151 are registered ports' and ports 49152 – 65535 are dynamic and private ports.

Question 8

Answer: A

Reasoning: Active Port Scanning is detectable by IDS solutions when TCP/IP ports are probed.

Question 9

Answer: C

Reasoning: Directive controls ensure compliance to security strategies, legislation, and regulations.

Question 10

Answer: D

Reasoning: The Bell-LaPadua Model has two simple rules that can be applied to access and integrity controls, though the context will determine the outcome. One rule focuses on information flowing or written to higher levels, while the other deals with the opposite direction.

Question 11

Answer: B

Reasoning: Access Deny is not a legitimate response. Access Reject is a response that denies access to all network resources.

Question 12

Answer: A

Reasoning: When dealing with port authentication on 802.1x networks, client software is not a required component of the process to restrict access through the ports.

Question 13

Answer: C

Reasoning: Honeypots are used to deflect attacks from valued assets on a network and allow patterns and behaviors of attackers to be studied.

Question 14

Answer: C

Reasoning: IP acceptance is not a phase of DHCP. There are four phases: the missing phase is IP Lease Acknowledgment.

Question 15

Answer: D

Reasoning: Static routing relies on manual entries from the network administrator. Link state and Distance Vector are types of Dynamic Routing.

Question 16

Answer: B

Reasoning: In a small office situation with the requirements stated, a passive hub would be sufficient. No external power source is required. Regeneration of the signal is not required since the office space is small, as long as the two farthest nodes are within the maximum distance for the cabling used.

Question 17

Answer: C

Reasoning: All other answers are applications of User Datagram Protocol (UDP). Email programs utilize TCP.

Question 18

Answer: A

Reasoning: Block and stream ciphers are the primary methods in cryptography using a combination of substitution and transposition. Block ciphers are usually found in hardware implementation, while stream ciphers are found in software implementations.

Question 19

Answer: B

Reasoning: The three essential practices of identifying users are uniqueness, nondescriptive, and issuance. All the answers provide a unique ID, except the first which provides a temporary account. The issuance of the ID(s) is similar enough as well. Having several accounts and IDs, especially for critical functions, provides the most secure option.

Question 20

Answer: D

Reasoning: Intrusion Detection Systems are a form of detective access control which identifies incidents or provided evidence. Web filters, virus controls, network operations and administration are other forms in the same category. The six categories are preventative, deterrent, detective, corrective, recovery, and compensation.

Question 21

Answer: C

Reasoning: VPN/VLAN are not authentication systems but include them in their solutions. RADIUS and TACACS are not generally considered single-sign-on solutions, but SESAME is. Other SSO solutions include Kerberos, NetSP, Kryptoknight and Snareworks.

Question 22

Answer: B

Reasoning: Asymmetric algorithms are not a specific device for maintaining message integrity but are used for message confidentiality through encryption.

Question 23

Answer: D

Reasoning: Real-time Transport Protocol defines the packet format used to deliver audio and video data over the Internet. Session Initiation Protocol is also associated with audio and video data but over IP, not Internet.

Question 24

Answer: B

Reasoning: The factoring attack attempts to break the RSA encryption method by factoring the product of two prime numbers.

Question 25

Answer: D

Reasoning: Firewalls are an IT technology that are typically found between internal and external networks for the purpose of preventing unauthorized access to an internal network. This is done by examining and filtering packets based on predefined rules. The primary purpose is still to prevent unauthorized access, not how the prevention is done or the access point where the filtering happens.

Question 26

Answer: C

Reasoning: Network Intrusion Prevention Systems can be connected to firewalls and are used to block unwanted processes received by the firewall.

Question 27

Answer: B

Reasoning: Classless Interdomain Routing (CIDR) is written using the IPv4 dotted decimal format with an additional suffix defining the number of bits used for the network ID.

Question 28

Answer: D

Reasoning: Spoofing pretends to be a trusted host on the network to create a connection that would have the victim send sensitive information to the attacker which can be used in a bigger attack.

Question 29

Answer: A

Reasoning: Assessment of Competition is not a valid step of OPSEC which includes five steps. The first and last steps are Identification of Critical Information and Application of Measures.

Question 30

Answer: C

Reasoning: VPN is supported by IPSec with mechanisms for authentication and encryption.

Question 31

Answer: D

Reasoning: When a wireless client moves from one access point to another on a wireless network, they are roaming.

Question 32

Answer: C

Reasoning: Talking is not a state definition used by ports utilizing STP. The five states are Blocking, Listening, Learning, Forwarding, and Disabled.

Question 33

Answer: B

Reasoning: The Take-Grant Model demonstrates the giving and taking of permissions between objects.

Question 34

Answer: C

Reasoning: Asset value and exposure factor are the contributing variables to determine single loss expectancy.

Question 35

Answer: A

Reasoning: NAT, or Network Access Translation, allows the use of private networks for organization. When a user connects to the Internet, a registered IP address from a pool of addresses is pulled to represent the private IP address on the Internet. PAT is a little more than simple NAT where the port number is communicated along with the IP address.

Question 36

Answer: A

Reasoning: Traffic shapers can be used to optimize network performance, lower latency, or increase bandwidth by delaying packets.

Question 37

Answer: C

Reasoning: Hardware devices that connect network segments together without any form of filtering or processing of the packet are bridges which operate on the data link layer. Switches can also operate on this layer or higher layers.

Question 38

Answer: B

Reasoning: The physical layer handles the 'physical' connections for the network. The data link layer allows data to be delivers across the link. Addresses in the frame aid the network layer in ensuring data reaches from the source host to the destination host The Transport performs error recovery and reorders the frames of the incoming data.

Question 39

Answer: D

Reasoning: Depth-in-depth solutions have two primary intentions: to force attacks to lose momentum or to spread out resources used by the attacker over a large area.

Question 40

Answer: A, D, E

Reasoning: The processes associated with access control and security aid in the planning, development, and maintenance of access controls in the environment. Change control ensures that changes, specifically related to managing risks or preventing attacks, are known and approved before implementation. Business Recovery and Disaster Recovery can identify requirements for access controls or vulnerabilities in the environment as it relates to maintaining business operations in the most critical situations. Performance Management establishes baselines that can be used to identify causes, such as attacks, to reduce performance in the environment. Other processes commonly associated include configuration, vulnerability or risk, product life-cycle, and network management.

References

Meyers, Mike. *CompTIA A+ PC Technician*, McGraw-Hill, Chicago: 2007.

CompTIA Network+ ExamObjectives. Computing Technology Industry Association: 2008.

Tipton, Harold F. and Henry, Kevin. *Official (ISC)2 Guide to the CISSP CBK.* Auerbach Publications, Boca Raton:2007.

Stewart, James Michael. *(ISC)2 SSCP Systems Security Certified Practitioner.* PrepLogic, Inc: 2006.

Certified Wireless Network Administrator Planet3 Wireless, Bremen Georgia: 2002.

Virtual Private Networks Administration Guide Version NGX R65, Check Point Software Technologies LTD: March 2007.

Online study guides:

www.ccnacertificationguide

http://www.mcmcse.com/cisco/guides/ccna_notes.shtml

GSEC information: www.giac.com

Websites

For more products, visit http://store.theartofservice.com/

For elearning, visit http://theartofservice.org/

Index

A

B

C

D

E

F

G

H

I

K

L

M

N

O

P

R

S

T

U

V

W

Z

CPSIA information can be obtained at www.ICGtesting.com
Printed in the USA
LVOW11s1404190415

435212LV00005B/473/P

9 781742 444352